i wasn't dead when
i wrote this

Also by
Lisa-Marie Calderone-Stewart

Faith Works series

Prayer Works series

Teens and Parents

In Touch with the Word series

i wasn't dead when i wrote this

Advice given
in the nick of time

Lisa-Marie Calderone-Stewart

LOYOLA PRESS.
A JESUIT MINISTRY
Chicago

LOYOLA PRESS.
A JESUIT MINISTRY

3441 N. Ashland Avenue
Chicago, Illinois 60657
(800) 621-1008
www.loyolapress.com

Cover illustration by Penelope Dullaghan
Cover Design by Jill Arena

Library of Congress Cataloging-in-Publication Data
Calderone-Stewart, Lisa-Marie.
 I wasn't dead when I wrote this : advice given in the nick of time / Lisa-Marie
Calderone-Stewart.
     p. cm.
 ISBN-13: 978-0-8294-3766-9
 ISBN-10: 0-8294-3766-5
1. Conduct of life. 2. Bile ducts—Cancer—Patients. 3. Calderone-Stewart,
Lisa-Marie. I. Title.
 BJ1589.C35 2012
 248.8'61969940092—dc23
 [B]

                                                                2012012308

Printed in the United States of America.
12 13 14 15 16 17 Versa 10 9 8 7 6 5 4 3 2 1

Dedication

I dedicate this book to my sons, Ralph and Michael.

You truly are my tomorrow's present.

Contents

Preface

Woody Allen once said, "I'm not afraid of death; I just don't want to be there when it happens."

I wasn't there when Lisa-Marie Calderone-Stewart died. (Yes, that's two hyphens, as she explained to me more than once.) But I was there with her just before she died, as we completed the book you're reading now.

As an editor, I've given authors outrageous deadlines before, but never one like I gave to Lisa. When I asked for this book, she had maybe weeks to live. What's worse, she had already submitted a completed project for my review. I considered that project carefully but decided against it.

Lisa and I were talking on the phone when I rejected her project. Then, ever so smoothly, I changed the subject and invited her to write something completely new.

There was a long pause. I wondered if she was angry with me—or just speechless at my audacity.

Finally, she said, "You do know I'm dying?!"

I said, "Well, yes, I understand—so we better get busy."

"You're serious?"

"I am, and here's what I want you to do . . ."

Lisa had spent a lifetime helping young people develop their leadership skills. She was a well-known speaker, had traveled all over the country, written books, and even earned her doctorate on the subject. Lisa's passion in life was reaching out to and training young people for success in life.

So I asked her to write her final message for the kids she would never meet. I wanted it to be serious but simple. I wanted it to sound just like Lisa sounded, as if she were having a conversation with a small group of young people who had gathered around her bed—well actually—it was more like a recliner love seat when we were working on this.

In my mind, I was thinking of a kind of *Tuesdays with Morrie* but with the possibility we might have only one or two Tuesdays to do it in.

Lisa turned out to be everything I could have hoped for, and more. We created a table of contents in one day. Then we argued about it for another day and finally agreed on format and structure. Then Lisa committed to writing a chapter a day. I committed to reading and doing an initial edit on each chapter as she finished them. In two weeks we had the basis of this book.

It's usually not this easy. I take that back—it's *never* this easy. I suspect it was a graced effort, and I believe Lisa was an exceptional person, maybe even a saint.

She decided that the project was worth doing, even as she suffered increasingly severe pain. To stay clear, she tried to hold back on her meds so she could write and edit with me. I'm not sure how she did it. Her visible pain was difficult to witness.

Lisa died shortly after we completed the book. Publication will be almost a year after her death. But what you're holding is Lisa's message of hope. Lisa believed in young people, believed in their abilities and their potential.

If you never met Lisa, my hope is that you meet her in these pages. If you did know her, you probably loved her, and my hope for you is that you hear her voice one more time and that it inspires you in some small way.

Joe Durepos
Chicago, Illinois
March 20, 2012

1

Not Dead Yet

On September 27, 2010, I was sitting in a chair in the third wing of Peggy House, an inpatient facility run by Center for Hope Hospice in Scotch Plains, New Jersey. I had sat in that same chair many times, right outside room 302, where my mother had lived for seven months. *This was the first anniversary of the day she died.* So after one year, I was back at the hospice, looking at the closed door of room 302. I sat there for at least an hour, not really saying anything to anyone.

Then I got up and headed back to my room, room 209.

I had started living at Peggy House at the beginning of the month. My room was in a different wing, but it had the exact same layout and color that my mother's room had had. Sometimes when I sat in my bed, I felt as if I were seeing my mother's world from the inside out. People looked at me the same way I used to look at her.

Mom entered Peggy House in February 2009. She had been diagnosed with breast cancer in the 1970s but went into remission until 2003, when it had spread to her bones and then eventually her brain.

I lived in Milwaukee at the time, and I flew home for a weeklong visit almost every month. I was in great shape in those days—I swam a mile two or three times a week.

But that same weekend in February, as we discussed moving Mom to Peggy House, I mentioned to my older brother, Joe (a doctor), how I'd begun feeling faint in the locker room after my swims.

In March, I was in Canada, giving a series of workshops, and I was amazed at how exhausting it seemed. I almost passed out in front of a group of several hundred people.

In April, I found a lump; in May, I had surgery; in June, they told me I had lymphoma. In August, a few scans and two biopsy operations later, they told me that I also had bile-duct cancer and would probably live only another six months or so.

My only chemotherapy treatment was around the time my mom died. I flew to New Jersey and attended her wake hours after the plane landed, but I felt terrible the next day. I had come all that way and was too sick to attend my mother's funeral! In fact, I was in no shape to return home to Milwaukee for almost a month.

I spent most of October living with my younger brother, David, and his wife, Rosemary. The Milwaukee hospital called me on my cell phone to say, "We are ready for your next chemo treatment," and I told them, "I haven't recuperated from the last one yet. I'm still in New Jersey, too sick to fly back."

I decided not to have any more chemo treatments.

I got back to Milwaukee just in time for Halloween, and I still felt pretty sick until December. My entire family came out to visit me, and we had a grand "last Christmas" that I will never forget. I expected to live only until February or March, but I was still alive in May 2010, when the intense belly pain began. Then they told me, **"Your time is running out. Time to fly back to your family while you still can, and die there."**

So I did. I packed up, and one son flew with me, and the other son drove my car. I took presents and love letters for immediate and extended family. We had several gatherings; I had the chance to give away all my stuff; and sure enough, in August, things got worse: increased pain, decreased energy, even a fever. I was dying. Time to move me to Peggy House.

I was prepared to die.
I was ready.
I did everything I wanted to do,
saw everyone I wanted to see,
and shared some wonderful good-byes.

They gave me some antibiotics, and my infection went away. I felt a little better. I started walking around a little more, and I even managed to start swimming again each week at a nearby YMCA.

On September 27, 2010, as I sat outside room 302, where my mother died, I started taking a look around at everyone else. I didn't look like them yet. But I knew my time would come.

But that's why you come to a hospice. Your medical team figures that you have only a short time left. So you come to die. It's your only job.

A month later, I was still alive.

I tried to let myself die, but my body just kept working. Not only was I still alive a month later; I didn't seem to get any worse. They did another CAT scan to see if I had been "cured." Nope. I was all loaded with cancer, worse than what my last CAT scan had showed. It was filling up my last remaining bile duct, and yet I was still swimming a quarter of a mile once a week.

My only job was to die.
I just wasn't doing my job.
They had to fire me.

My doctor in Milwaukee saw the CAT scans and said, "Wow. If it were anyone else, I'd say this patient with this cancer in her liver has maybe a week or two left. But you? I won't predict anything anymore! If you are still swimming, you don't belong in a hospice! Why don't you come back to Milwaukee if you want to?"

I thought that was a great idea. I had tried dying, but maybe I should go back and try living again.

So I was home in Milwaukee in time for Thanksgiving.

I didn't feel great, but I did feel a little better. I managed to have friends over. We even went out to eat once a week or so. A friend of mine moved into my little condo so I wouldn't be alone.

I had another Christmas, another birthday, another Easter, another summer, and I still wasn't dead yet!

September 27 has just passed me by again. Two years since my mother died. This time, I couldn't visit room 302. It's been almost a year since I got my pink slip from the hospice. I still can't believe it.

I don't expect to live much longer. Seriously, the pain is pretty bad. I am exhausted most of the time. I go out far less often, and I truly can't imagine that I have many more months left.

But you know what? I can't complain! I have had a great run of it. I've outlived the original six-month prediction and passed the two-year mark. I've had lots of fun these last two years. People have been great—visiting, calling, e-mailing. It's like that vacation I always wanted to take (except for the pain).

Having terminal cancer really makes your life easy.

No one expects anything, so the bar is very low. I was in the pool a few months ago, and someone told me that I had an "awesome backstroke." In my entire swimming career, no one would ever in his or her wildest imagination evaluate my backstroke as "awesome," but suddenly, because I have terminal cancer, I'm rocking the aquatic world with my athletic skills!

The folks at Loyola Press asked me if there was anything I'd want to write about before I die. I laughed at first. "Are you serious? I might not be alive long enough to finish the table of contents, never mind writing a whole book!" They said, "OK, just try."

So I tried.
If you are reading this, then I finished it.

This is it—my last book.

I should be careful about saying that. I thought I wrote my last book a few months ago. Nope—that wasn't my last book. That was my second-to-last book. I can't imagine there will be another one after this one . . . but who knows? Like my doctor, I won't predict anything anymore.

2

Go Find Your Best Self

"Whether you think you can, or you think you can't—you're right." Henry Ford is famous for saying that. In other words, if you don't have the self-confidence to do something, you probably can't, even if you can.

A Matter of Confidence

It was September 22, 2000, at the Summer Olympics in Sydney, Australia. **The officials setting up the equipment for the all-around women's gymnastics competition did something very careless.** By mistake, they set the height of the vault to be two inches too low. Their error wasn't discovered until eighteen of the thirty-six women had already competed.

Some of the athletes who had been scoring high all along received low scores on the vault because of the vault's incorrect setting. But at the time, no one realized the error. According to an article in the *Milwaukee Journal Sentinel*, "Those with low scores, such as Elise Ray of the United States and Svetlana Khorkina of Russia, were demoralized beyond rescue." ***Demoralized beyond rescue***—that is quite a description.

Headline News, an online news service, described the event with these words:

> [Svetlana Khorkina] was leading after the first rotation. But she didn't get nearly enough height on her first vault and was still rotating when she crashed onto the mat on her knees. Tears already were filling her eyes, as she got up, knowing she'd probably just lost the gold [medal]. She nailed her second vault, but the damage was done. When a coach tried to

comfort her, she angrily pulled her arm away and stomped off. Her confidence shaken, she fell on the uneven bars. On a somersault over the bar, her fingertips brushed the bar, but she wasn't able to grasp it, plunging to the ground with a thud.

Svetlana Khorkina had been in first place. Her level of competence had not been reduced. She was still capable of champion-level accomplishments. She was still the best of the best.

But her perception of her competence had changed. And therefore, she was not able to perform to her ability. **She was "demoralized." Her "confidence was shaken."** She didn't think she could, so she couldn't—even *though she really could.*

See how important confidence is?

And see how easily it can be shaken? Svetlana no longer felt like a champion, and in every event that followed, she fumbled, she fell, she missed her mark.

Our Fragile Lives

Most of us are so fragile inside.
The smallest things can take away our
confidence.
It doesn't even take a big thing.

When I was in second grade, I spent a lot of time writing valentines for all the students in my class. The teacher gave us a list of names so we wouldn't forget anyone. On Valentine's Day, when all my classmates gave out valentines, I waited to receive mine. Everyone else had a pile on their desk. At the end of the distribution, I had received exactly one valentine. One! How could that happen? **Only one person in the whole class wanted to send me a valentine.**

I ran home in tears. When I got home, my mom saw how upset I was, but I didn't want to tell her what happened. Finally, she got the truth out of me. You'll never believe this, but when she was in second grade, she received only one valentine, too! Isn't that amazing? She could actually say to me, "I know just how you feel!" (Something you should almost never say, because it's almost never really true.) She hugged me and cried with me and told me her story.

I got to thinking about how my mom had tons of friends and a wonderful husband (my wonderful dad), and how she was smart and pretty and worked at my dad's office. And she had received just one valentine in the second grade. That meant there was hope for me! I could still grow up to be happy, smart, and have friends! Hearing her story made me feel better, less hopeless, and more confident.

Illusions and Delusions of Popularity

Something I didn't realize when I was a kid but know for certain now: being popular in school is not always a beneficial thing.

Popularity often teaches kids how to be manipulated by a crowd. It can encourage you to

- downplay your uniqueness
- sacrifice your principles to maintain your social status
- make decisions on the basis of what other people want instead of what you want, need, or know

Popularity might even teach you to have a sense of entitlement, as in, "I am better than other less popular students, so I deserve more." That kind of thinking can be dangerous; it can lead to all kinds of poor decisions.

Yet . . . **being *unpopular* teaches you resilience**, self-reliance, independence, self-respect, imagination, and creativity, not to mention other values that are more pure and timeless—and less dependent on current trends.

So if you are "unpopular," fear not!

Lots of actors and musicians were unpopular in high school. Many "nerds" and "geeks" grew up to be inventors and technology wizards. Hang in there. Keep looking for that friend or two who might be the type to have sent you your only valentine in second grade.

Try to find some activity you like, and go develop that interest.

Think about what you enjoy doing, and search for opportunities—a service organization where you can volunteer or a business where you can find an adult to mentor you in a skill or talent. Often, a nonpaid internship can turn into a paying job later on.

If you are one of the popular ones, then be more careful with what you say and do. Avoid anything that might be the least bit like bullying. Watch out that you don't look down at those "unpopular" people. Chances are, one of them will end up being your boss or, at the very least, your competition for a future job. If you really want a challenge, try making friends with someone you think is very different from the types of people you usually hang out with. Try volunteering at a soup kitchen, a food pantry, or a community center.

The fact is, many people who were the most popular in school have a harder time later.

Consider this: if you are smart, good-looking, and athletic, and everything has always come easily to you, you will tend to overestimate your future success and happiness and to underestimate the amount of work and sacrifice it will take to get there. If you've always had to try harder for every accomplishment, you know all about making the extra effort. You will be just the kind of employee some boss will be looking for.

About Beauty . . .

I am completely amazed that the fashion industry is able to brainwash not only young people but adults as well—and to do it so easily. Somehow a few voices—fashion "authorities"—manage to convince millions of people that a particular style is in this year but out next year.

People not only obey the "rules" of fashion; they pay a lot of money to keep up the appearance of being fashionable. They are even willing to be uncomfortable and unattractive, in their search for this high status! I have seen people walk long distances in shoes that are killing their feet and in styles that do not flatter them in any way, just because it's the latest fashion.

And what about all the "product" we're encouraged to wear in our hair and on our skin? You're actually afraid to hug someone because it might smudge your makeup or knock your hair in the wrong direction.

These things become traps. They limit what you do.

They prevent you from just being and doing, without having to first consider the fashion implications!

A True Story

Once I found two pairs of designer-label shorts in a thrift store. They cost me five dollars each. I bought two identical pairs. I removed the label from one of them. When I wore the ones with the label, I would get all kinds of compliments. When I wore the others, no one said a word. What's wrong with this picture? We can't tell whether or not a garment is acceptable unless there is an actual sign sewn onto it indicating, "This is one of those cool brands. Proceed and purchase with confidence."

When I insisted that my plain shorts were a high-status item, no one believed me. Then I would whip out the tag I had removed and show them the identical shorts that still had the label sewn on.

Sometimes this led to embarrassment on the part of the nonbelievers. But other times, they just didn't get the irony. "You ruined the shorts by removing the label!"

I wanted to say, "No, actually, you are ruining your sense of style by allowing yourself to be manipulated by companies who charge too much money and trick you into thinking that you can be a better person just because you have some word or logo stitched onto your pocket or lapel!" Of course, I never said anything like that.

The bottom line:

- *Clothes don't indicate anything about your importance.*

- *You are more wonderful than any hair gel or makeup.*

- *Your talents are more spectacular than any fashion trend.*

- *You are more brilliant than your ability to accessorize.*

> I only wish I could get you to believe it—to truly believe it.

Set a Trend!

During my professional life, I tried very hard to convince people that fashion was an illusion. For instance, I hated high heels—they hurt my feet. I never bought any. I also didn't care for tight, revealing clothes—I noticed that people dressed that way tended to draw more attention to their appearance than to what they said and did. So I wore clothing that was more loose and comfortable. I didn't like the way nylon stockings felt. They were hot in the summer, not warm enough in the winter, and they ran easily and cost a lot of money. I stopped wearing them.

I flew around the country giving workshops and training all kinds of people in leadership skills, and I would wear suits and dresses with nice (flat) shoes and anklet socks.

I wore only styles that flattered me. Some of the clothes I wore were recent purchases, and others had been in my closet for five years or more.

Do you think anyone had less respect for me when I showed up and gave my talks? They still applauded, bought my books, and asked me to come back and give more workshops. And they complimented me on my "unique style."

In fact, two female lawyers I know stopped wearing nylon stockings! They met me for lunch, showed me their low-heeled professional shoes and their anklet socks, and said, "Look! I'm hooked on the 'Lisa' style! I should have started this years ago!"

Now, if you love the feel of nylon stockings, go ahead and wear them—and enjoy them!

My point is that you will be surprised at your freedom when you start making decisions on the basis of what's comfortable for you, what's practical, and what's economical.

Why do you think the fashion industry keeps changing the rules? To get us to keep buying entirely new wardrobes. There's nothing wrong with replacing your wardrobe—but it should be because you really want to, not because you feel pressured to be in style.

Be comfortable.
Be the real you.
Don't be duped by marketing.
Don't insist on always being the first to buy the latest and most spectacular.

You will also be surprised at how much more attractive you become when the only fashion rules you follow are the ones that make sense for your life. These are rules you write, not rules imposed on you by anyone else.

Embrace the Adventure!

Life can seem so overwhelming.

What a chore, what a bore, to have to constantly make decisions, negotiate your way through conflicts, and forge new paths around so many obstacles.

But what an adventure!

Please, embrace the adventure! It can be so difficult to stand before the challenges of life and think, "I can do it!"

It's especially hard to find that self-confidence on those really awful days when everything goes wrong and no one seems to have faith in you.

But I am begging you to do exactly that. **It's our only hope for a better world.**

You might not believe it today as you read these words, but you are a miracle. No one else has ever lived on this planet with

- The same set of talents and abilities you have
- The same way of thinking and problem solving
- Your delightful laugh, with your exact sense of humor
- Your amazing soul

Don't waste a minute of your life regretting who you are or wondering why you couldn't be some other person. You are just what the world needs now.

Please, find that best self inside and live confidently:

- Be more responsible than your parents expect.
- Study more than your teachers require.
- Show more respect than the students in your classes are used to.
- Do more than anyone asks of you.

It doesn't matter if you can't be the most athletic, or the smartest, or the most popular. You can be the kindest and the most fair. In today's impolite world, that's rather easy. And it goes a long way. You will be astonished with how the universe responds. I promise.

3

Love and Be Loved

My mom taught me this at a very early age: when you think kindly of someone, let them know. **Don't waste an opportunity to communicate your positive feelings.**

So when I thought about a relative I hadn't seen for a while, I would write a note. When my mom was driving me around doing errands, and we passed a flower shop, we would stop to get a flower for a dear friend living nearby. It was just a way of life.

Good Tippers

My dad was always a big tipper when we ate out. He did more than order a meal; he established a relationship with the person taking our order—just to be nice. Why not?

> It's always more fun to be nice than not to be nice.

When my son Michael was younger, he would notice how large a tip I would leave. He would tell me, "That's too much."

I'd remind him of all the people who don't tip very well, or not at all, and how hard it is to walk back and forth all day, carrying heavy trays and hearing mostly complaints from people who treat you like a servant instead of a fellow human being. Once he became a waiter, he understood! He couldn't believe all the times he got no tip at all.

He's a big tipper too now!

Begin a Flood of Goodwill

You can begin a flood of goodwill with anyone who serves you with his or her business. Think of it—mechanics, hair stylists, bank tellers, receptionists, people at the front desk of the YMCA. Their doing a job well makes my day.

And how many people really tell them that? Usually, they hear complaints or nothing at all.

I started this habit many years ago; I would bring cookies or brownies or a jar of candies (or even a dozen donuts) whenever I had my car serviced or my hair done or a physical checkup. Just to say, "I appreciate what you do for me." You would think I was giving out gold. I used to bring similar goodies to work once a month or so, to share with my office colleagues as well.

It's so easy to share joy. There's no good reason not to do it.

The last time I had a procedure done for my cancer, I packed up several big jars of candy. Not just for the doctors and nurses, but especially for the staff at the lab and at radiology. They were my first introduction to this illness, this new identity for the rest of my life. Before I ever met my first oncologist, I met the folks who drew my blood and took pictures with the big machines.

I hate needles. They always make me cry. So that first person with that pointy thing is the most important person of the day. The way the lab techs do their job makes all the difference in the world. They hold my hand, look in my eyes, and tell me, "We're going to take good care of you," and they mean it. Often, that technician will never see me again, but I still get treated like royalty.

Same thing with the CAT scans. The people in radiology don't just throw you a medical gown and say, "Put your arm here. Hold your breath."

They call you by your name; they ask how you are doing. They touch you in a way that's somehow calming and comforting. They know the whole experience is frightening.

They ask whether you're comfortable, if it hurts, if you can handle one more pose or if you want to rest for a minute—they apologize when something hurts.

They don't get the big bucks. But they do get to experience all the patients who are grumpy, or angry, or so frightened that they only know how to react by being grumpy or angry. **They do their best with every difficult personality they encounter.** We patients walk in, filled with anxiety and fear and confusion, and we often walk out feeling braver and more confident, because someone really cares about whether or not it hurts to "put your arm here" or "hold your breath" one more time. They have the power to make me feel like a piece of meat, poked and prodded, with a chunk removed and labeled. Yet, instead, they make me feel cared for, comforted, protected—even loved.

I think they deserve a whole lot more than a jar of candy.

Care Is Paying Attention

Even your close friends—maybe especially your close friends—need to be reminded of what makes them special to you. **When you see your friend go the extra mile for someone, or forgive someone instead of holding a grudge, or step up when someone needs a favor, it's important to say something.** "That was a good thing you just did. It's just one more example of why I'm proud to be your friend. You inspire me. Thank you."

One time, when my son Ralph was in high school, he was invited to a birthday party, and he had no extra money to buy a gift. I made a suggestion that he thought was ridiculous. He decided not to go at all rather than go without a gift. Then the girl called, to be sure he was still coming. He was kind of trapped, so he said yes and then reconsidered my gift idea.

I told him to think of all the things he liked about this girl, remember the time he spent with her, and think of "symbolic" household items.

I even helped him gather some: a marble, a paper clip, a rubber band, a seashell, an eraser. He wrapped each one separately, with a note:

- "This marble reminds me of how you can just roll with it when things don't turn out perfectly."

- "This paper clip symbolizes how you manage to hold it all together and stay so organized."

- "This rubber band is like you because you can be so flexible when your friends need you."

- "This seashell reminds me of the time we walked by the lake last summer."

- "This eraser takes away all the mistakes; you are forgiving like this eraser."

His present was the hit of the party; no one had ever received anything that took such thought and care. **Cost of materials: $0.00. Value of his message: priceless.**

Getting Serious

Relationships that become exclusive and intimate can be a real puzzle to some people: teenagers, newlyweds, even couples married for ten years or more. The real secret to keeping a romance going is to *keep the romance going.* To never stop trying. To never develop the attitude, *"I have this person's eternal admiration, so I can stop trying now."*

Always act as if you are still starting out, as if you are still trying to win over his or her heart.

Because in a long-term relationship, that's what you need to do. No one wants to be taken for granted. No one wants to feel unspecial.

What do we want? We want you to keep winning our heart!

Romance is nothing more than the fun of being loving—
the delight of expressing your appreciation for the other person.

The more loved you feel, the more creative you become.

When you are in a healthy relationship, it will help you become a better person. You will enjoy the world more, and your partner will, too.

Romance doesn't need to take over your life—it doesn't need to be fake or phony—and it doesn't need to be a stressful chore. If it's that difficult, maybe this isn't the right person for you.

Romance comes naturally when you become less selfish and more considerate; less preoccupied with everything in your life and more interested in the other person's life.

Romance means being more curious about what the other person thinks and feels, to know and understand him or her better. It means asking a lot of questions and really caring about the answers.

Communicate, Communicate

Unfortunately, according to the statistics, females are better at asking questions and listening than males are. But it makes sense. In the beginning of our civilization, the women stayed home, took care of the children, cleaned out the cave, and cooked the meat over the fire. They chatted and communicated all day long. Those skills were very important for females.

The males were out and about, quietly stalking the animals they would kill and haul back to the cave. They couldn't talk much, or the animals would hear them and run away. Men did things side by side, without saying much. Those skills were very important for males.

But now, the rules have changed. Both males and females are expected to know how to communicate with words and how to work together silently, depending on the situation. And in a faster-paced world, there are so many opportunities to misunderstand one another.

The skills of precise talking and careful listening are more important than ever.

Think of your favorite television show or movie. Most likely, there are several misunderstandings that lead to unnecessary arguments, sometimes fights, and the eventual disintegration of a relationship. Until somehow, the stubborn one finally gets an insight and accepts another point of view, or the lying one finally confesses and is forgiven, or the hurt one finally clarifies the reason for the recent silent treatment and receives a complete explanation.

The best way to approach what looks like a deliberate hurtful action is to say, "I feel [hurt, disappointed, disrespected, whatever you feel] when you [describe whatever the person has done], because then [describe the negative consequences] and what I really want is [whatever it is that you want instead]."

I used to teach this formula to teen leaders I worked with. One of them went off to college, and she remembered that formula from our leadership training. She made a big poster for her room:

> #1. Careful Talking:
> I feel . . .

When you . . .
Because then . . .
And what I really want is . . .

#2. Careful Listening:
I hear you saying . . .

Every time she had a conflict with her roommate, she pointed to the poster and insisted that both of them use the formula. It always helped them resolve their differences. Word got out around the dorm. Students she didn't even know would show up, knock on her door, and say a little sheepishly, "We heard you have some poster or something that helps people solve problems . . . Do you have a few minutes to teach us how to use it?" She quickly became very well-known; it wasn't long before such posters were appearing in the hallways of the dorm.

The Best You Can Do

When you find yourself in conflict with someone, it's best to assume that the other person just didn't have all the information necessary for making a good choice, that the other person has a good heart despite his or her most recent apparently heartless action. Look for the best in the person. Do this while listening very carefully to the words and paying attention to body language and tone of voice.

Sometimes, though, while talking to a person, you realize that he or she
isn't as interested in your concerns as you thought,
or isn't mature enough to handle an honest discussion,
or isn't willing to keep a relationship healthy and life-giving,
or isn't capable of being dependable (because of drugs, drinking, illegal actions, or affiliations with friends who are a negative influence).

In that case, it's time to say that you care very much for that person, but you can no longer continue the type of relationship you had hoped for. It's just not going to work out the way you thought it would.

You might be sad, very sad, for a while. **You might feel incomplete and lost and in need of some half of yourself that seems to be missing.** But it's always better to be alone for a while and to stay healthy than to remain in an unhealthy relationship just to avoid being alone. It never feels that way at first, but it always feels that way eventually.

If you are loving and honest with all your friends and in all your relationships, even when you need to challenge someone, you will never need to regret what you said or did, or to be ashamed of your words or actions. When you handle situations with respect and patience, you can be at peace.

Then There's Sex

First of all—just trust me on this, OK?—it is not a good idea to casually hook up for sex instead of dating and building a real relationship.

"Hooking up" is a dangerous trend, on so many levels.

What's funny—in a sad kind of way—is that young adults who want to avoid getting hurt think they can be perfectly happy jumping in and out of bed without really caring about the person they are with. Physical intimacy seems easier and safer than emotional intimacy.

You can try that for a while, but sooner or later, you will do some serious damage—to yourself or to the other person.

The most obvious consequence is catching one of many sexually transmitted diseases. **Medically speaking, sleeping with someone is like sleeping with every single partner that person ever slept with.** One word: Eeewwww! If that's not enough to convince you, do a Google search on STDs. There are probably several you've never even heard of. Before you know it, you'll be saying "Eeewwww!" yourself. Out loud.

Another possible consequence is that you will start to care anyway, in spite of yourself.

You won't avoid getting hurt. You will get emotionally involved, even if you think you won't—even if you really try not to.

You will start to feel lonely even when you are with someone doing the very thing that is pretty much the opposite of loneliness. You will get very hurt, even though you started doing this to avoid getting hurt. Even worse, your hook-up partner could start to care and then get hurt. The suffering you cause this person should break your heart.

And if it doesn't break your heart, then that's even worse. That means you have managed to ruin the most amazing, marvelous, phenomenal physical human activity in the entire cosmos by removing everything that makes it amazing, marvelous, and phenomenal. And that benefits you . . . how, exactly?

Lovemaking—or Button Pushing?

So, if sex is so amazing,
marvelous,
and phenomenal,
why don't more people experience it that way?

Sometimes, one person thinks he knows just what the other person wants. So that person rushes to deliver, and the other person doesn't know how to respond to the disappointment.

Just because you know what buttons to push doesn't mean you know how to be a sensitive lover. It's not a race to push the buttons. **Lovemaking is all about finding the most loving and sensitive and fun and creative ways to make contact.**

Otherwise, lovemaking becomes a business transaction. You don't feel loved and cherished. You feel like someone whose buttons are being pushed so you can both get to the finish line and declare the race over.

Some people truly believe that's all there is to lovemaking.

Well, that's all you need to know to make babies. And it's quite possible that for some people who approach sex from a basic, selfish standpoint, the only satisfaction they require is to finish pushing the buttons.

But everything isn't a race. The main purpose isn't to get to the finish line.

Once, I went to the movies with a guy I really liked. When the kissing started in the movie, of course, I started to feel a little "warm" inside. I was suddenly aware of how we were sitting; my right hand on my right leg wasn't far from his left hand on his left leg. His knees were practically touching mine. Then he shifted his weight and our knees touched. Then I shifted my weight and our pinkies touched! He immediately moved his pinkie against mine, I moved mine against his, and then he took my hand.

We didn't talk about this first date until a few weeks had passed. He said I was the one who took his hand first!

He was wrong. But I dropped the subject. About an hour later, I just let my pinkie brush against his pinkie, and he immediately took my hand.

I asked, "Who just decided to hold hands right there?" He told me, "You did."

"See," I replied, "this is what happened that first night at the movies! I did not take your hand! I just barely touched you, and you sensed that I was open and so you responded by wrapping your hand around mine. So you are the one who started the actual hand-holding!"

He protested, but I think the point is obvious:

When two people are ready for affection, then the slightest indication on one person's part is perceived as an invitation.

We might call it the initiating event, even if it's unintentional or accidental.

Touchy, Touchy

I think this is how children in the backseat of a car start fighting: "Stop touching me or I'll hit you." (Later, there is an *unintentional* touch, followed by *intentional* hitting.) "He hit me for no reason!" "You touched me!" "I did not!" and "You hit me on purpose!"—all followed by parents' intervention.

> When two people are ready to fight, the slightest indication (even if it's an accident) is perceived as a threat.

And the other person feels justified in making a return strike, even if the first strike was completely unintentional.

So who really "starts" it—the first one to do something intentional? What if someone pretends it's unintentional, and the other person is certain he or she is pretending? Hmm . . .

In an unhealthy relationship, people seem to be looking for reasons to fight and argue. They don't trust each other, so any action or word that can possibly appear to be negative is assumed to be an intentional attack. And each person is already poised to match each attack (real or imagined) with a counterattack. If the first person didn't say or do anything on purpose, the counterattack seems to come out of nowhere. "I was just walking along, and somehow this pebble was kicked up and touched your foot. Next thing I knew, you were hurling boulders at me!"

People in unhealthy relationships never seem to understand what they are fighting about or how the fight even got started.

It's a red flag. It's a warning sign. It's time to end the relationship.

The Dance

Things are very different in a healthy relationship. It's like the knee-knee, pinkie-pinkie, hand-holding thing from the movies. You make a small move, hesitantly at first, as if to ask me the question, "This?" and then I respond with my body in a way that gives the answer, "Yes, this!"

A healthy relationship is like a gentle dance, and it accomplishes a lot.

First of all, it's a delightful reminder for us to slow down and enjoy each other. Sometimes, we think we know where we're going, so why ask for directions? But when we always rush to the destination, we often miss the scenery along the way. Sometimes the scenery is the best part. Sometimes the best part of loving is being reminded that your partner is crazy about your scenery.

Second, the gentle dance gives each of us a chance to say, "You are so beautiful. It is such a privilege to be with you. I am so honored to touch you in this way. I am so thrilled to witness this part of you. I am so lucky to be with you," but without using words.

When two people communicate this adoring message to each other on a regular basis, their trust and appreciation for each other deepens.

And because the purest message of love is communicated so consistently, minor misunderstandings are easily forgiven and forgotten.

(See how different this approach is from the business transaction? "OK. Here we are. We both know how to push the buttons, so let's just do it.")

Or consider a jealous, arrogant point of view. "You are mine, and I am doing this because I have the right to do it. And it's your job to enjoy it and thank me for it."

This controlling manner is the opposite of love, but if it's the only attitude you have experienced, then you might begin to think that it's the only way things are or could be—and that it's your fault for not being satisfied.

Third, the gentle dance gives both people a chance to steer the direction of what happens. You may think you know exactly what I like, but my mood tonight might be different from what it was last night. (Your mood could change, too.) I might welcome more of this and less of that. By doing the gentle dance of "This? Yes, this!" we are also open to the possibility of "This? Hmm, no, not tonight . . . but how about this?"

Fourth, you can always agree to steer things toward becoming more intense. But starting off gently and going through the dance is always the most romantic way.

Lovers who practically live on the wrong side of "harsh" can't imagine this. And those who long for the gentle dance often don't know how to explain it. You can't do the gentle dance without being gentle.

Gentleness Is Part of Any Healthy Love

I think many women instinctively communicate in a gentle way, because nonverbal body language is the essence of how mothers interact with their babies. They need to say, "I love you more than my own life" without using words. Watch a mother with her newborn. She constantly kisses him or rubs her nose on the baby's skin. She touches his arms and legs or kisses her tummy.

She sings, she rocks, she prays, she giggles. She does everything possible to say, "You are so beautiful. I am so lucky to be with you. I will protect you and love you and give you all the best."

She does it all gently, and she watches to see what the baby enjoys. When the baby giggles with delight, she does more of that thing. When the baby gets fussy or acts uncomfortable, the mom notices right away and stops doing whatever got that response.

A lot of fathers are good at this communication too. I've seen them play the gentle dance with their babies for hours. But for many people, there's a learning curve when it comes to gentle love that pays attention.

Of course, sexual love with a partner is not the same as parental or family love for a child. But the concept is the same; in both situations, people use the gentle dance of love.

New friends might use the same dance when they are figuring out which movie to attend. You don't want to be too forceful and suggest a particular show, so you might ask, "Romantic comedy or science fiction?" Your friend may counter with "Science fiction or action drama?" and then you go back and forth before suggesting a particular title. It happens all the time.

But some partners are clueless. They don't know how to do the gentle dance. You can teach them, but only if they have a gentle heart. Here's another reason for two people to be in a committed love relationship before they take their clothes off.

Other partners are worse than clueless; they are abusive. When your partner tries to control you, manipulate you, and/or threaten you, you are being abused. This can be emotional, or it can be a combination of emotional and physical. If ever you find yourself in such a relationship—even if you think you should be afraid—then please, run away.

And understand this very clearly: rape is not sexual activity. It is an act of violence. It is a crime.

Rape counselors often say, "If you hit someone over the head with a frying pan, you wouldn't call it cooking."

So there are all sorts of reasons to build an intimate, safe, committed, exclusive, love relationship with someone before you get into bed! I can't emphasize this enough.

Let me end where I began.

Casual sex will never bring you that most amazing, marvelous, phenomenal physical human experience in the entire cosmos.

Happily married couples will tell you that in a New York minute. It's the gentle dance that makes it happen. Stronger passion can always evolve (and it often does), but if you never do the gentle dance, then that deepest passion never really comes at all. And all you get is just a race, with a finish line—and really, no winners.

4

Family Is Hard—So Work at It

When I was in high school, I really wasn't a great daughter to my parents. I wasn't really a great sister to my brothers. Even though we are a very close family now, I still have regrets about what I was like back then.

I'm not talking about major trouble;
there were no drugs,
no jail,
no pregnancy,
no drinking while driving,
or anything illegal like that. I was just . . .
selfish.

And not very considerate.
And not always respectful.

My mother said it was harder to raise me than to raise my
three brothers all put together, times a hundred! We used
to joke about that, whenever we were with someone who
said, "It's harder to raise girls than boys, isn't it?"

But when you pressed my mother for examples, she
couldn't remember any details—just general teen angst.

Reality Check

I remember hearing my parents talk about me one morning during my senior year in high school. ***My mom said, "I don't know what happened. Lisa used to be so sweet. What happened?"*** My dad said, "I can't figure it out. It's as if we lost her somehow."

Their words broke my heart. I wanted to come flying down the stairs and say, "No! No! You didn't lose me! I love you! I'm sorry!" But I was frozen. I didn't move or say a word.

I thought the only way I could change was to wait until I was in college. Once I was away for a month or two, and they came to visit me for Parents' Weekend, then maybe they could see that I was different, and they could accept the new me.

That's exactly what I did. They took me to college in mid-August, and we said good-bye. I said, "I'll see you for Parents' Weekend," and my roommate teased me and said, "You'll never last that long! You'll want to go home before that." But I knew I couldn't enjoy the luxury of visits home. I had to stay away long enough for my parents to believe I had changed.

When Parents' Weekend came, I had presents for my parents, and I had written a love letter for each of them.

I had completely cleared my schedule, so I had nothing else to do all weekend except what they wanted to do. I didn't even have to study or write a paper or anything. **My only plan was to show them the ideal daughter.**

It worked! We didn't have any need to argue or fight, and I went along with whatever suggestions they had. I did all the things I'd wanted to try months earlier, when I was afraid they would think I was faking it. None of it was hard to do at all! I just treated them the way I would have wanted someone to treat me.

At the end of the weekend, my mom said to me, "I can't believe how much you have changed in just a couple of months!" My dad agreed. "It's been so long since I had this much fun with you!" he said.

Mission accomplished.

Real, Permanent Change

That was the beginning of the rest of my relationship with my family. If you ask any of my brothers, they hardly remember that selfish, self-absorbed, inconsiderate sister they had for a couple of years. They think I exaggerate about *how* bad I was as a teenager.

When my parents were both alive, I called at least once a week, maybe more. I wrote them letters and notes at least once or twice a month. After my dad died, I called my mom even more often.

My parents were my biggest fans. They truly believed I could do just about anything I put my mind to. They taught me marvelous lessons, guided me through life's ups and downs, and supported me no matter what happened.

I adored them, admired them, enjoyed them, and now I miss them both very much.

During those two or three years of the different me, I don't really know what got into me. But whatever it is, I know it happens to lots of teenagers.

I was incredibly lucky. My parents loved each other very much, and they loved all of us kids.

Finding Home

Many factors make family life much more difficult to negotiate. When there is a single parent, or a missing parent, a parent in jail, a parent who drinks or does drugs, an abusive parent, or a parent with some other mental health issues, it's almost impossible to have a "healthy and normal" family dynamic at home. Home might not be safe. "Home" might not even actually be your real home. I know many young people who are raised by their grandparents or other relatives.

Rules differ from family to family. There might be things you are not allowed to talk about. There might be a lot of fear and tension at home.

What works in the normal and healthy world doesn't work in a home where things are unsafe, insecure, and dysfunctional.

If you are in a family situation like that, I hope you are able to find a father figure, a mother figure, a safe adult, perhaps even a safe family, to be your home away from home—a place where you can be yourself, where you can be honest, and where you can be comfortable.

Every teenager needs a place with adults who care about you and can give you advice and assist you with problems that you really should not try to tackle on your own. This is especially true if you have younger brothers or sisters you are worried about.

You may be in a healthy home but one that's been traumatized by a recent tragedy. Maybe someone close to you has died or someone at home has a disability or a terminal illness.

> # Even though your family may have its hands full dealing with the most pressing issues, you still have needs, yourself.

It's OK to lean on some trusted family friends for a while; you don't have to shoulder the burden of your heavy feelings all alone. Please promise that you will do that for yourself if your family is going through a difficult time.

Parent Issues

One thing I have learned is that issues with your parents will be issues all your life, until you resolve them. **Parents are such a *huge* part of who you are.** If there is a rift between you and your parents, please find a way to heal it. Here are a few possibilities.

1. You might need to change things. You might especially need to change yourself.

When I was in high school, I realized that I'd done some damage to the relationships with my parents and family. When I saw what I was doing, I decided then and there to stop my immature behavior.

So I did. **I stopped being selfish and started being considerate.** I started treating my family the way I wanted people to treat me. It was so easy once I recognized what I needed to do. I only wish I hadn't waited until college.

A lot of parents have complained to me about how their sons and daughters never talk to them anymore. They just come home, grunt greetings, stay in their rooms attached to their electronic devices, and then go out. They stay home just long enough to find something to eat and change their clothes. These parents love their kids and would do anything to "have them back" in a closer relationship.

You don't have to become best friends with your parents. But the very least you can do is be nice. You know what I mean: nice.

Be thoughtful.
Say, "Good morning."
Tell them "Thank you" when they do something for you.
Hug them.
Tell them, "I love you."
Every so often, tell them what you like about them or what you admire about them.
Once you start, it's easy to keep it up.

Thanks, Dad. You really are a good cook. I know it takes time to make supper. I want you to know I really appreciate what you do for me.

Thanks, Mom. I really appreciate the ride. You're so organized; you somehow manage to get all your errands done and help me with mine too. I appreciate that.

2. You might need to apologize.

Instead of waiting until I was in college, **I wish I had just written *my family* a letter, apologizing for my nasty**

and inconsiderate past and announcing, "Today was the first day of the rest of my life as *your-less-selfish-and-more-appreciative* daughter." I could have brought them flowers and marked the day on the calendar. I just didn't think of it at the time.

The important thing is that you communicate very clearly in your letter (or "speech," if you want to do it in person) the following points:

- Admit that you have been at fault for doing this or that or for not remembering to do this or that. Give examples of what you are referring to.

- Apologize for what you have done. Apologize for not treating your family better. Apologize for not being grateful for all they have done for you. Make it clear so that they know what you are sorry about.

- Explain how things are going to change. Give specifics. "I will be more cheerful. I will spend more time talking with you every day. I will not complain as much. I will help out with [fill in the chore: laundry, meals, cleaning, dishes]."

- Mean it and do it! You must follow through. You must show them that you really are a new person. You must be that new person.

After one week, sit down with your parents and ask, "How is it going? Have I changed? Am I doing the things I said I would? Is there something I'm still doing that you really hate?"

And listen to what they say. You will truly knock their socks off! Keep meeting with them every week, for maybe a month. And then maybe you can meet once a month.

You will remember this as the best thing you ever did for your parents. And years from now, your parents will tell this story about you. They will talk about the transformation you brought to your family, entirely on your own. You will become a legend in your own time—within your family, and maybe even in your neighborhood!

3. You might need to forgive.

It's possible that you are in one of those difficult situations I mentioned earlier—with a parent who is missing either physically, emotionally, or mentally. **It might be that you have so much anger inside** that you spend lots of time taking your frustration out on others.

You can't ever be at peace if you have issues with your parents that you refuse to resolve.

Even if you have a missing parent who is not willing or able to apologize to you, you can still forgive him or her. You can even forgive yourself if your missing parent will never be able to hear a direct apology from you.

Do you think I am overemphasizing the role that parents play in our lives? Check out the statistics on people in prison and their family situations: *More than 90 percent* **of men in prison had absent fathers when they were growing up.**

It's hard to know what parents go through until you have your own children. Once I was responsible for taking care of my sons, I remembered my parents in a whole new way. And when my oldest son and his wife started their family, he thought of me differently too.

You will be amazed at what you are willing to do for this tiny new life in your arms. You will never believe that you could ever love anyone as fiercely or as faithfully. **You will be willing to fight bears or pirates or even spiders, with your bare hands, to keep this child safe**—*whatever* it takes.

And wait until you find out what it takes!

You discover a lot during the first few months, when you are sleep deprived and it seems that every smile, every frown, every cry, every burp, and every poop dominates your life as much as any significant work deadline or world crisis.

Imagine someone spending so much time fussing over you when you were a baby—it's something to think about.

True Stories

When my younger son was in college, he went through a rough time. I'm not sure why, but all of a sudden, his grades dropped, he wasn't studying, he started smoking and drinking, he was going out with friends who dragged him down with their own irresponsible behavior, and he found himself spending a lot of time coaching them on how to clean up the messes they kept creating.

Naturally, I was concerned. I kept reminding him that he couldn't lose his scholarships.

He couldn't afford to let his grades drop anymore. Without those scholarships, we would not be able to pay his college tuition.

He really needed to get his act together.

All of a sudden, he did. **Everything changed.** I have no idea why. Many times I have asked him, "What happened to you? What made you change?" All he could say was, "I guess I just grew up. I realized I needed to be different. So I started doing what I needed to do."

In a matter of weeks, all his habits changed. We still can't explain it. But it convinces me of this: when you want to grow up, you can.

You don't have to remain selfish, immature, ungrateful, and lazy.

So if that's what you are, then simply change. Grow up. We know you can do it. And you know it too.

Another time, my older son was planning on getting together with his girlfriend for her birthday. Her best friend would also be there, with the best friend's boyfriend as well. They planned this for weeks—he was so excited.

The big day came—and there was a blizzard. Schools closed at noon. It continued to pour down snow the rest of the afternoon and all evening.

But my son kept begging us to let him drive over to his girlfriend's house. **I did everything I could to convince him how dangerous it was, but he didn't care.** He insisted he would be careful. I reminded him that, just hours ago in the daylight, before an extra foot of snow had fallen, it had taken me forty-five minutes to go three miles on main roads that were plowed. He was expecting to drive on unplowed side streets, in the dark. No way.

Then he asked if he could walk there. If he cut through all of our neighbors' backyards, it might be only a thirty-minute walk. I still thought it was too dangerous. He offered to stop in at three houses along the way. We made the phone calls. Everyone agreed.

The plan worried me, but we let him go. The neighbors and I checked in by phone to be sure he was progressing and hadn't collapsed in the snow someplace on the way.

He left around supper time and returned before nine o'clock that night. When he returned, he said to us something like this:

"Thank you for not letting me drive tonight. I could not believe all the crashed and abandoned cars I saw on the road. I could have been killed. I almost didn't make it coming back. Checking in with all those neighbors? **Seriously? I thought you were crazy. But it probably saved my life. I just want to say that tonight I learned that maybe you are a better judge of certain situations than I am.** I learned a lot. I want to apologize for all the times I have been nasty because you didn't let me do something I thought was perfectly fine. I just want you to know I really love you."

I had tears in my eyes. I said, "Would you do me a favor? Would you repeat that speech to your younger brother?"

A voice came from the top of the steps, "I heard it."

Maybe you will be wiser than I was, and you will be able to resolve your issues with your parents while you're still living at home with them. Please do it. I wish I had.

I'm very fortunate to have had a spectacular relationship with my amazing, talented, brilliant, loving, affectionate, supportive, terrific parents.

Do what it takes—apologize, forgive, change, love. Do it today.

If you're lucky enough to live with your parents, go give them a hug.

5

Say What You Mean and Mean What You Say

I used to ask teenagers about lying. I'd ask, **"Is it OK to lie?"** They would always answer, "Of course not."

I would ask, **"Do *you* lie?"** They would say, "Of course we lie—or we'd never get to do the stuff our parents don't want us to do. Of course we cheat, or we could never keep our grades up. Everyone cheats."

Really? Everyone? Seriously? *Everyone?*

Well, not everyone, and not all the time. But it can sure seem like that.

I used to ask them if there could ever be a good reason—a really good reason—to lie. A reason even God would approve of.

The one example people most often come up with is this: Let's say you are hiding innocent people from some bad guys. Let's say you have a Jewish family hiding behind a secret panel in the basement. If the Nazis come knocking on your door and ask you, "Do you have any Jews in here?" then you are allowed to say no. God would not require you to say, "Yup, down the steps, second panel on your right."

In that case, you are not really lying. In that case, the words take on a different meaning. These soldiers would not be merely inquiring about the well-being of your friends. **In code, they are essentially asking you, "Will you cooperate with us in our senseless murder?" and you are truthfully saying *no*.**

Those situations are rare. ***Most of the time, the lies we tell are so unnecessary.*** But half the sitcom plots on television are based on some lie told in the first few minutes that leads to more and more ridiculous lies to cover up the first lie, until the whole thing unravels, and toward the end of the show one person asks the obvious question:

Why didn't you just tell me the truth?

While I was visiting a family once, I saw one child tell her friend to shout bad words into a new toy microphone. The child's mother corrected the boy, saying, "We don't say words like that here." He innocently pointed to her daughter and said, "She told me to."

"I did not," she protested. Then she gave me a look as if to beg me to defend her and lie for her. Immediately her mother looked at me. "Did she tell him to say those words?" I had no choice—I had to tell the truth. I nodded yes. The girl completely denied doing it, saying I was the one lying. She stormed off to her room and was angry with me for the rest of the evening, insisting that I had lied on purpose. Even the next day, when I brought it up, she refused to admit to the truth. Somehow she had convinced herself that what she was saying really happened. I found the whole situation very disturbing.

> Usually when I ask teenagers for the number-one reason they choose to lie in a situation, they answer, "To stay out of trouble."

When I ask for the number-one reason they choose to tell the truth in a situation, they answer, "To stay out of trouble."

I come from a family of pathetically honest people. We can't even lie when we are trying to keep a surprise birthday party secret. All of us—my three brothers and I—blush, stammer, and look away. We'd be putty in the hands of the FBI or the CIA; no lie detectors necessary!

I kind of like being this way. It's easy to trust me. **I like being believed.** There's something wonderful about knowing that whatever I say, people assume I am being honest.

Character Matters

Once, when I lived in Saginaw, Michigan, a person from the bishop's office came to visit me. **He asked me if I told a group of teenagers from a neighboring parish to ask their pastor to fire their youth minister.** I laughed. Then I noticed he wasn't laughing. I said, "Is this a serious question?" He told me that, yes, the youth minister had accused me of putting them up to the task of getting her fired.

"Of course not," I said. I did remember that they had come to a retreat I'd led recently, and they were upset at their youth minister for some decision she'd made. I suggested they go back and talk to their youth minister and share their feelings and thoughts with her. They said, "She won't listen." I said, "Give her the chance. If you try to talk, and she won't listen, then go back with some of your parents, and maybe she'll listen then, because you will be demonstrating how serious you are about your concerns." That's all I told them.

He told me, "I thought it might have been something like that. She accused you, so I had to come and ask."

"Is that all? Am I in some kind of trouble?"

"No, I have no reason to doubt your word. I believe you."

I used that story for years, with my own sons, with my nieces, with teenagers in several states.

He had no reason to doubt my word. Why? Probably because he couldn't remember me lying about anything.

He believed me because in the past I had shown myself to be an honest person.

It gets better. After Saginaw, I lived in Nebraska. Years later, I was looking for a job in Milwaukee. **Guess who interviewed me?** The same man who had trusted me in Saginaw. He became my new boss.

See how important it is to be honest and trustworthy?

I tried to impress this upon my own two sons especially. "What if you are accused of doing something bad at school, something you didn't do? When you explained that you didn't do it, would anyone believe you?"

All it takes is one lie from your past—just one lie—and your reputation for honesty is weakened. The teacher, the principal, even half the students could very reasonably say, "We heard him lie before, so why should we believe him now?"

A Snowflake Has Six Points

When I was in grade school, our art teacher had us fold white paper in half and then in half again. She gave us scissors and had us cut out sections and then open the whole thing up. "Look," she exclaimed, "a snowflake!"

I came home and did the same thing for my mom. I folded paper in half and in half again. After cutting, opening, and saying, "Look, a snowflake!" I could see my mother's serious frown.

"Who taught you that?"

"My art teacher."

"Your art teacher? Oh my goodness."

My mother was disappointed. Snowflakes have six points, not four. It's not all that hard to fold paper in half, and then in thirds, and then in half again. When you do that, and you cut out the sections, you get a six-pointed snowflake. My mother taught me this immediately, and I practiced all afternoon. The next day, I was instructed to show my snowflakes to my art teacher and explain what my mother had said about real snowflakes having six points. I was a little scared of the whole confrontation. But my teacher was delighted. She wrote a note home to my mother and asked her to come into class and demonstrate this.

I learned something about being authentic that day.

My mother was authentic. Say what you mean and mean what you say. If it doesn't have six points, then it's not a snowflake. **Don't say it is if it's not.**

Either change what you say or change what you do. If you want to call it a snowflake, then make sure it has six points. If you want to just stick with your four-pointed design, then call it a cutout, or a symmetrical shape, or a four-pointed design, but don't call it a snowflake.

I also realized what a good teacher I had. Instead of feeling insulted, she took the opportunity to learn from someone who knew more than she did. She was humble enough to learn from a student. And she cared enough about being authentic that she invited my mom to teach everyone herself.

You really can't go wrong when you strive to be authentic.

Never be phony,
never be fake,
just be yourself,
no matter what.

When you're authentic, you don't have to pretend to be better than someone else. It's OK if they are smarter, more skilled, or more talented—nobody's perfect. You know what you're good at, and you can recognize what other people are good at. Sometimes you will get to teach something you know, and other times you will get to learn from someone else what they know.

Authentic Is the New Cool

Once I was doing leadership training with a group of young people I didn't know. I had barely begun when I realized there were two guys in the back row clearly making fun of me. I started to ignore it, but they weren't stopping. **So I walked to the back of the room and said to them, "Hmm. I believe you are making fun of me."** They were caught off guard, and they didn't really know what to say.

They looked down and didn't respond, but I could tell I was embarrassing them. Naturally, I really didn't want to make them dislike me; I wanted to make friends with them.

So I was trying to get to what was true about this situation (always a good thing, looking for the truth); I was merely being authentic.

I told them, "Even from across the room, I could look at you two and see that you are both pretty cool guys." Shy but hesitant smiles began to emerge. They didn't want me to trap them and end up making them look even more foolish. But they didn't know me yet.

They had no way of knowing that my goal was to make them feel more comfortable, not less. So I continued.

"Even from across the room, I bet you two could look at me and think that I, on the other hand, am not all that cool. Am I right? Is that pretty much what you were thinking? It's OK to be honest. It won't get you into any trouble." They still had no idea what to say. There was confusion in their eyes, even though their embarrassed smiles were trying to cover for it. "I bet on my best day, I'm not as cool as you are. Hmm, yes, I'm sure of it. **You are more cool than I am, even on your worst day.**"

By now, half the room was giggling, because they didn't know what to expect.

I turned to the class and insisted, "Am I right? It's probably true, don't you think? I mean look at them and look at me? No contest." Then I turned back to the two boys. "But here's the thing. You are stuck with me for the whole day. From the other side of the room, I could tell that I would probably learn something important from you today."

I am just asking you to give me a chance and see if maybe you might learn something from me, too.

"I mean, why not just try it out? Besides, I brought candy. And I give candy to all the students who participate. I might give you a Jolly Rancher for having a jolly attitude. I might give you a peppermint patty for a really refreshing insight. I might give you a roll of Smarties for showing me how smart you are."

By then, they could not contain their grins and laughter. "OK, it's a deal," said the first. "Are you serious about the candy?" asked the second one. "Yes I am." He said, "OK.

If you brought us candy, just to get us to pay attention and learn something, I guess that's a pretty cool thing." **I held up two Almond Joy bars from my pocket for the class to see.** "This is because I think you two are going to bring a lot of joy to our group today."

(I always bring candy to my leadership training sessions. It's a great way to encourage participation. And most people—young and old—enjoy the silly comments I make about the candy. "A Mr. Goodbar for a Mr. Really Good Answer.")

I had no idea how that was going to turn out. I was just winging it. But I figured, what did I have to lose? They already thought I wasn't cool. I may as well state the truth and see if I could at least get them to cooperate with the uncool teacher for a day.

When you're authentic, you don't have to worry about being cool. Being cool doesn't matter.

Or maybe being authentic is a deeper level of cool. Maybe it's the most radically, astonishingly, sweetest cool there is.

Being a "cool" person of integrity means more than just being a person who avoids lying. You have probably heard people say, "Practice what you preach," or "Don't talk the talk unless you walk the walk," or "Actions speak louder than words." **It's not always easy to be a person of integrity.**

Surprising Outcome

I used to teach nonviolent conflict-resolution methods to high school teenagers in the city of Milwaukee. I would train them to present these same peacemaking skills to groups of middle schoolers. It's still going on today; twice a year, the Teen Leaders of Tomorrow's Present teach a workshop to middle school youths called "Hope Is Something You Do."

A while back, one of the freshman teen leaders showed up at practice Saturday morning, and he didn't look all that happy. I asked him what the problem was.

> *"I almost got into a fight yesterday because of you."*

"Because of me? How did I do something to get you into a fight?"

"Because I wanted to fight. **I wanted to punch somebody's lights out.** And I could have. He was this stupid bully picking on my little brother. I wanted to knock him across the room and give him a lesson he'd never forget."

"And so what happened?"

"You know I couldn't do it."

"Why not? He was bigger than *you*?" (This was a big, strong dude.)

"No. Because I'm on your peacemaking team. My brother knows I'm on your peacemaking team. I couldn't fight in front of him. Boy, was I mad at you."

"So what did you do?"

"I had no choice. I had to use all that stuff we teach the kids at our workshops. You know, the careful talking, the careful listening, the 'suggestions for how to solve the conflict.' All that stuff."

"And?"

"And it worked. We worked it all out. Nobody had to punch anyone."

"So, I'm confused. Aren't you happy about being so successful with your leadership skills?"

"I guess so. It's just that I never believed it would work. For three months, I've been coming, and for three months, I've been thinking, 'This stuff will never work.' And I was so ready to prove it to you."

Then when I couldn't punch the bully who was picking on my own brother, and I did the stuff we teach, and it worked, and I realized I had been wrong all along.

"I hate being wrong."

By this time, the other young people had arrived and they had been listening to his story.

One of the senior girls took over. "So let me get this straight. You thought our stuff wouldn't work. You were forced to act like a peacemaker because your little brother looks up to you. You used our stuff. **You solved the problem.** You were a great role model for your brother. You showed everyone here that you really learned it well, that you're a leader and a person of integrity. Do I have the facts right?"

"Yeah, that's about it."

"And you're mad at Lisa because she was right and you were wrong, because you didn't believe our stuff would work?"

He started to laugh. "When you put it that way, you make me sound ridiculous."

"If the shoe fits . . ." She just threw up her hands and walked away. Everyone caught the irony. He should have been feeling proud and happy and confident and satisfied with a job well done. He finally realized why everyone was laughing and he said, "Actually, what I did was a really good thing. And besides, if everyone did what we teach, we wouldn't have to worry about bullies threatening our little brothers in the first place."

In spite of himself, he had become a person of integrity. He just wasn't prepared for how that felt inside.

Integrity Leads to Doing Right by the World

Usually, there's something pure and natural about integrity. It feels good to be authentic, because it's you to the core. No need to be a bully, no need to prove you can beat up a bully, no need to lie, no need to worry about people not believing you.

Children easily catch on to this sense of fairness at an early age. You hear them utter, "No fair!" at the first hint of anything that is unjust toward them.

Unfortunately, the world is not fair. People aren't all born into ideal situations.

Some children are lucky enough to be born in hospitals, to healthy mothers, who have been watching their nutrition, exercising moderately, and taking good care of themselves to help their babies come into the world as strong and healthy as possible. **Some children are less lucky.** Their mothers abused drugs or alcohol, or their fathers abused their mothers, or they were born in a bathroom and left to die before someone else found them. Or maybe their mothers and fathers did everything possible to ensure a healthy birth, but somehow their child was born with some kind of disease or limitation.

Some children are born into free countries, where most citizens are safe, and the water is clean, and food and clothing are abundant, and they have indoor plumbing and electricity and books and toys. That would probably describe most of you reading this book. **Do you realize how lucky you are?**

Many children are born into poverty, in places where there is no clean water, no plumbing or electricity, very little food, oppressive heat, lots of bugs and germs, lots of sickness, and very little hope for improvement. They often don't get to learn how to read; even if they survive long enough to reach their fourth or fifth birthday, there are no schools for them.

It's hard to believe that more than 24,000 people die every day from hunger-related issues.

That's eight times the number of people who died on September 11, 2001—dying every day.

It's easy to see when things are unfair to us. It's not as easy to realize when things are unfair to others.

One problem with looking at justice in the world is that we tend to get overwhelmed. **How can I help 24,000**

people every day? I can't. I simply can't. I can barely get my homework done and my teeth brushed, you might think. Between being overwhelmed and feeling guilty, some people decide to ignore the injustice of the world and hope it goes away.

It will never go away.
So why bother?

I'll tell you why: because people of integrity bother; they care.

They see something that's unjust. They take time to learn about it. They think about what they'd like to do, what they can do, what will help—and then they make a plan. Then they do what they plan, and they see if it helps. If so, they do more of it better. **If not, they fix what doesn't work.**

Even a Child Can Do It

My niece Elizabeth was in second grade when she saw a television show about children and hunger. She asked her parents about it. "Do we have hungry children in our neighborhood?" They assured her that the children in their neighborhood were fine, but other neighborhoods nearby did have some hungry children.

All by herself, she came up with an idea. Her birthday was coming soon, and she had planned to have a birthday party and invite every student in her class. **She asked her parents if it would be OK with them if she told her classmates to bring food instead of birthday presents.** That way, they could take all the food and bring it to the hungry children in the other neighborhoods.

It became a yearly tradition. The folks at the local food pantry got to know Elizabeth very well. After she brought her first birthday food collection, they weighed it so she could write to her friends and tell them how much they collected and how many meals it would bring to other families. Every year, they would beat the record of their previous year. She and her family started bringing food during other times of the year as well.

Do 24,000 people still die each year
from food-related issues?
Probably.
But does Elizabeth make a difference
with her service?
Absolutely.

When she gets older, Elizabeth will probably become more interested in issues of hunger and poverty. Giving food to hungry people is excellent service; even better is finding a way to prevent the people from getting hungry in the first place.

What's happening in those neighborhoods
where the families can't provide enough food for
their families?

Is the economy bad?
Did parents lose their jobs?
Is there not enough affordable housing?
Is there a sick person in the family?
Do the adults have to choose between paying the rent,

buying medicine,
and spending money on food?

People like Elizabeth who are concerned can become economists, social workers, lawyers, or community organizers. They might become doctors, nurses, pharmacists, or researchers. They can become civil engineers or city planners. There are all kinds of ways to address the issues that lead to poverty and hunger. They could become stay-at-home moms and dads who volunteer with organizations working toward social change.

A Simple Exercise

If you still think everything seems hopeless, I invite you to do a simple exercise.

On one side of a piece of paper, try listing all the problematic issues you can think of—things like hunger and poverty and sickness and homelessness and bullying and illiteracy and abandoned pets and rape and gang violence and war.

On the other side of the paper, try listing all the agencies and organizations that are already working on these issues. Things like soup kitchens and food pantries and homeless shelters, and shelters for battered women and their children, and hotlines and research foundations for every disease you can think of, and the Red Cross and Doctors without Borders. The list of agencies and organizations ends up being longer than the list of issues.

Why would I ask you to do such a thing?

Because people of integrity are people of service and justice. It's one thing to say you care about people; it's another thing to show it. There are countless opportunities.

You don't have to save the world. You only have to find one area in which you can serve.

Once you start serving, you will learn more about that issue. Then it will become part of you; you will start thinking about it—thinking about how you can contribute, thinking about your own skills and talents. You'll make a plan, and you'll follow through and see if it works. If it works, you'll do more of it, and you'll do it better, and you'll get some of your friends to join you. If not, you'll find ways to fix what doesn't work. And you will still get some of your friends to join you. And you'll make new friends who are already involved in the same justice work. And together, you'll support one another as all of you learn more, and you'll reflect more and plan more and serve more. Before you know it, you'll be a leader.

Service . . . learning . . . reflection . . . leadership . . . support . . .

That's what people of integrity are all about. That's what people of justice do. And they do it together, with other people who care. ***Because none of us can accomplish anything alone.***

This is the honest truth. It's the coolest thing you can do with your life.

And it's as authentic as six-pointed snowflakes.

6

Stay Curious and Use Your Imagination

My youngest brother, David, is very curious. In fact, ever since he was little, I have always given him Curious George items: stuffed animals and coloring books when he was a child, T-shirts and gym bags now that he's an adult. He is also a scientist, just like the man in the yellow hat, Curious George's companion.

Wherever I go with David, he's always looking around. When he sees a pipe hanging from the ceiling, he follows it to see where it goes. When he sees a mechanical device, he studies it to figure out how it works.

> He has taught me to be more curious with my observations and more precise with my language.

My whole family leans toward the scientific. My oldest brother, Joe, majored in chemistry, and my middle brother majored in physics. Both of my parents majored in chemistry. When I was in high school, my chemistry teacher wrote this in my yearbook (it is the only signing I know by heart): "I hope someday, somehow, the great god of chemistry can impart to you the knowledge which I could not."

With all the knowledge floating around our house, oozing from the brains of my brilliant brothers and parents, there was yet something higher in priority: imagination. The genius Albert Einstein (1879–1955) is famous for saying:

Imagination is more important than knowledge.
For knowledge is limited, whereas imagination embraces the entire world,
stimulating progress, giving birth to evolution.

Imagine that! To be able to imagine something is more important than just being able to know something! For instance:

- Early one Saturday morning, I came downstairs to find my dad at the kitchen table, arranging toothpicks. **He was just playing around until he had an idea.** By arranging the toothpicks, he figured out how he could build a table out of wood, with two sections that would fold down and become seats. First he imagined it; then he got so excited, he made that table bench before the weekend was finished.

- When I was in school, my mom kept reminding me to always learn "the basics," to have well-rounded knowledge and a healthy curiosity about different things. She forced me to take piano lessons when I was in grade school and sewing classes in high school. She encouraged me to take a music history class and an art history class in college. She promised me I would never regret it. She was so right! I'm not particularly talented in any of those areas, but learning those things trained me well for all my life.

- When we were kids, our parents always had us make cards and presents instead of buying them. I still love making things. My sons, nieces, and grandsons have many storybooks that I have written for them about their fictional adventures. **I would use photographs of their heads and then draw in their bodies doing all kinds of courageous and exciting things.**

- When my sons were young, they made Christmas presents every year as well. My boys learned to make latch-hook rugs, to sew pillows, to do needlepoint, and to glue and paint on any texture. They made angels; St. Nick figurines; doorknob decorations; wreaths; and all kinds of ornaments with wood, glass, plastic, and fabric. They learned how to read instructions, follow directions, and assemble items in stages. We spent hours watching Christmas specials and football games, working together with our craft supplies spread out on the floor.

• Every December, we used to spend one day working on cookies and crafts. We built things in the living room, baked things in the kitchen, and the kids switched back and forth to avoid boredom. But every other year, it seemed to be a disaster. We'd run out of something at a crucial time, or get tired and frustrated and yell at one another, or step on somebody's project, or trip and knock over and break some significant item. Ralphie even ran away from home for several hours on cookie-and-craft day. We found him by suppertime, sitting in our backyard! By then, it was dark—I think Michael found him when he went out to feed the dog. Not too long ago, I asked them about cookie-and-craft day memories, and I was prepared for the worst. But they had totally forgotten everything negative that ever happened! According to them, we were the perfect family, right out of a Hallmark holiday movie. **All they remember are the fun**

times and the great stuff they made. Go figure! I'm grateful for that kind of imagination!

Advice Worth Noticing

My dad used to tell me to stay curious, so I would always keep learning. It was great advice. He also told me never to underestimate a situation or a person; if I stayed open-minded, I would be surprised at the kinds of situations and people who might be able to teach me something important.

He said some people are too stubborn to learn from anything or anyone. The only way for them to learn is to make their own painful mistakes. And then sometimes, they still don't learn!

> My dad said that if you have to learn a lesson the hard way, you pay a high price.

He called that **the tuition of life.** But if you are shrewd enough to learn from someone else's mistake, he called that a scholarship, because you got the lesson but somebody else paid the price. And if you are clueless enough to make the same mistake twice, that's like failing the class and having to pay tuition again to attend summer school.

For this reason, I have always stayed curious, always observant, always willing to listen to what people had to say about life—I especially like hearing their life stories. I am always looking for a life scholarship.

I could never understand young people who proudly proclaim to their elders, "Just let me make my own mistakes!" That seems like such a foolish attitude! Why pay all that tuition when there's a scholarship right in front of your nose?

You don't have to take someone's advice, but it sure is silly not to listen to it and at least factor it in with everything else you consider before you make a decision!

Ask Questions

When my sons were younger, every time they were making a decision, large or small, I'd ask them a bunch of questions. I usually didn't have a preference as to what they decided, but I wanted to be sure they were thinking it through.

Sometimes they would get frustrated and say, "Why don't you just tell me what you want me to do?"

I would have to convince them that as long as they had really good reasons for what they were choosing, I would support their decision. I found myself saying the same exact thing my dad used to say to me when I was young: "I'm just trying to make you think!"

Once in a while, my sons might have been planning to do something foolish, but after some serious discussion time ("What is your situation or problem? What is your overall goal? What are all your options? and What are the pros and cons of each option?"), it became quite obvious to them which options were foolish and which were wise; the solution just surfaced after all that good thinking.

They learned to be very good decision makers.

Now when I need to make a decision, I call upon *their* wisdom and expertise. They usually end up walking me through the same process I taught them as kids—only they can often imagine more options than I can, and they can imagine more pros and cons than I can. See? Imagination is more important than knowledge!

How to Teach

I like to tell people, "I can teach you to teach anyone." I created my method, the Four Gs of Teaching, to teach high schoolers and even middle schoolers how to teach others.

Think of all the talks you need to give throughout your education; think of all the times you need to give reports, summaries, or do group teaching experiences. This method is foolproof, because it is based on the learning cycle, which is what professional educators recognize as the most natural way we learn.

Here are my Four Gs of Teaching:

1. **Grab my attention.**

2. **Give me something new.**

3. **Get something out of me.**

4. **Go make a difference.**

How do they work? I'll walk you through an example.

Let's say you and a friend want to teach some middle school students about solving conflicts with the EASE method. Here's what you could do, using the Four Gs:

1. Grab my attention.

You might start out with a cheer. Everyone knows how to do "Give me an E!" ("E!") "Give me an A!" ("A!") "Give me an S!" ("S!") "Give me an E!" ("E"!) "What does that spell?" ("EASE!") "Yay!" (Everyone cheers!) And now that you have their attention, and they have already learned

EASE, you can tell them they will soon know how to solve conflicts and problems with EASE.

Ask them if they know what *ease* means. (If they don't know, make the question even easier: if you do something with ease, does that mean it's easy for you, or does that mean it's difficult for you? They will usually get the answer right when you ask it that way!)

2. Give me something new.

Now, do a skit. You and your friend can act out being a busy parent and a kid who overslept and forgot to get some special school supplies together. It's morning, it's late, both of you are trying to negotiate eating breakfast as well as finding cardboard tubes and masking tape. Both of you get frustrated and angry, and then you scream and insult each other. (Keep it clean but authentic.)

Ask them if anyone has ever been in an argument like this. Tell them they will now learn how to handle these situations with . . . (if no one calls out "EASE!," you can start that cheer again.)

Tell them that EASE stands for "Explain, Admit, Suggest, and End." (It helps to have a poster or handout.) Have them repeat that: explain, admit, suggest, end.

3. Get something out of me.

E = Explain. Say, "In this part, each person needs to explain how they felt and what led to their frustration. Who has a suggestion? What kinds of things should the parent say? What kinds of things should the son or daughter say?"

Thank them for their suggestions. Then demonstrate a good "explain" segment of the EASE process:

Parent: "I feel frustrated when you sleep late and don't tell me until the last minute that you need extra supplies. Because then everything is rush, rush, rush, and what I really want is for you to be more organized."

Kid: "I feel overwhelmed with everything I have to do for school. I was up so late studying, and I'm still exhausted. I feel worse when you yell at me, and what I really want is less pressure."

A = Admit. Say, "At this point, each person needs to admit their own role in making the situation worse. It should also include an apology. Who has a suggestion? What kinds of things should the parent say? What kinds of things should the son or daughter say?"

Again, thank them for suggestions but challenge them for thoughtless comments. Then demonstrate a good "admit" segment of the EASE process:

Parent: "I hear you saying there's too much stress. I'm sorry for making it worse. I admit that I hit the snooze button too many times, and I always feel as if I'm running late, too."

Kid: "I hear you saying I shouldn't do things last minute. You're right. I'm sorry. Last night I knew I needed those supplies. I admit that I said some really nasty things to you. I'm really sorry about that, too."

S = Suggest. Say, "Now, each person suggests what they can do to make things better. Who has an idea? What kinds of things should the parent say? What kinds of things should the son or daughter say?"

Then demonstrate a good "suggest" segment of the EASE process:

Parent: "What if you made a list as soon as you got home of everything you need to do before going to school the next day? I can look at it as soon as I get home, and we'll make sure everything is done before either of us falls asleep. Will that work?"

Kid: "That will help. What if I cleaned my room top to bottom this weekend, so it's easier for me to find stuff. I know I had a roll of masking tape someplace."

E = End. Say, "This just means that you keep making suggestions until each person is satisfied that they have come up with a workable solution."

Demonstrate it:

Parent: "Thanks for being so open about talking this through. I feel better."

Kid: "I feel better, too. Thanks for understanding." (Hug optional.)

4. Go make a difference.

Have each participant turn to one person and talk about a real conflict at home and how they will use the EASE process to resolve things. Then after everyone has talked, ask the group members to share their plans. Thank them for the attention, and ask them one more time, "What are the four parts of EASE?" Help them recite: "Explain, admit, suggest, end." Have them all clap and applaud themselves for a job well done.

Let's Recap

Be curious. Imagine. Create. Keep Learning. Try teaching.

Don't forget that fourth G: ***Go make a difference!***

We need all of you brilliant teenagers to spread your knowledge—even more important, your imagination. Teach us well. Some of us want to keep learning all our lives. The day we stop learning is the day we die. (Well, even then, I bet there's more to learn!)

Imagination is more important than knowledge. For knowledge is limited, whereas imagination embraces the entire world, stimulating progress, giving birth to evolution.

—Albert Einstein

7

Learn from Teenagers and Small Children

Most things we learn, we don't really set out to learn. **The learning happens while we're busy just *doing*.**

Never Say "It Can't Be Done."

I was never a jock. I was always chosen last for kickball. I can't dribble a basketball while moving forward. I have never hit a ball with a bat. But somehow, I could always swim without drowning.

I was planning to be a kindergarten teacher, so I got a job as a summer camp counselor. I was told, "Next year, the only available job at the camp will be the head swim instructor." I said, "OK. I'll take that job."

"What? You're a lifeguard and a swim instructor?"

I didn't see the problem. "No, not yet. But I will be, by next summer, if that's what you need."

Raising of eyebrows, rolling of eyes, laughter. "Don't be ridiculous! No one can do that! It can't be done!"

You don't tell someone in my family "It can't be done." That's one of the trademarks of being a Calderone. The only possible response is "Watch me."

I took some Red Cross courses at the local YMCA. First semester, I became a lifeguard; second semester, I became a water-safety instructor. No problem. For the rest of my college career, I spent my summers teaching children to swim.

Why Didn't I Quit?

During my junior year of college, my roommate convinced me to join the Holy Cross swim team. The team had twenty slots, and only nineteen people tried out. That's the only reason they kept me on the team. **I came in dead last in every race I ever swam—every race.** Usually, I swam only the fifty-yard freestyle: dive in, swim to the wall, flip turn, swim back. By the time I was doing my flip turn, everyone else was out of the pool. No kidding. I swam one entire pool length all alone every time. Every swimmer I ever met was at least twice as fast as I was.

> Why didn't I quit? I don't know! I enjoyed swimming. I kept improving, reducing my time by two or three seconds each race.

Here's the best part: Senior year, the only other senior on the team dropped out. I received the Outstanding Senior on the Swim Team award—no one else was eligible, so they had to give it to me! They gave me a Holy Cross watch!

No, actually the really best part was that I got a job coaching a swim team.

Finding My Leaders

I was a kindergarten teacher during the school year and an aquatics director and swim-team coach during the summer. In Montgomery, Alabama, where it's so hot, the only summer job I could imagine was at a pool.

It was a YMCA summer-league team.

Nobody had Olympic dreams—the point of the program was to keep kids occupied during the summer.

Parents wanted their sons and daughters to become safe swimmers, and the kids just wanted to have fun.

During my first two summers, the assistant coach pretty much ran everything. His kids were on the team; they were jocks, and he was a jock. **So who was I to question his expertise?** We won about half our meets.

Then the jock family moved out of state. It was up to me. I would have to be the real coach, not just the one who did the paperwork. *Yikes!*

I really didn't know what to do, so I turned to the experts—the teenagers on the team. (The team included boys and girls, between the ages of six and seventeen.)

We had a leadership meeting, and I asked them these questions:

- **What have you loved about the swim team?**
- **What have you hated?**
- **What would make it more fun and a better team?**

They came ready to talk, and I came ready to listen. They had criticism; they had praise; and most of all, they had creative ideas. This was exciting! We put together a brand-new plan for our swim team. **The kids became my leaders, my assistant coaches.**

For years, I looked back at that imaginative, resourceful, honest, committed group of teenagers, and wondered,

"How did we manage to create such a successful and fun swim-team experience—especially with a coach like me?"

I learned the answer to that question almost twenty years later, when I did a three-year research study on what made teenagers want to be leaders. Guess what: the teenagers in Milwaukee, Wisconsin, said the same kinds of things that the teenagers in Montgomery, Alabama, had said. Not only that, I discovered that some of the leading experts in business and education were beginning to say the same things as well!

I will tell you what I learned about leadership from listening to teenagers.

Wisdom from the Water

My kids' first observation was that the meets took too long. They were all-day affairs.

We didn't just have a butterfly race. We had boys' butterfly, age eight and under; girls' butterfly, age eight and under; boys' butterfly, ages nine and ten; girls' butterfly, ages nine and ten, and so on.

The youngest kids got bored, lost track of time, sometimes forgot what stroke they were swimming—and sometimes they missed a race completely!

We couldn't actually make the meets shorter, so they thought of a way to solve the major problem. **Their first great idea was to assign every swimmer a buddy.** Each seven- to twelve-year-old partnered with a thirteen- to seventeen-year-old. The older buddies had to know their younger buddies' schedules, go get them during the meet, stand in line with them, cheer for them as they swam, and hand them their towels when they were done.

At that first meet, as they stood in line, the older buddies passed the time by quizzing them on the upcoming race. It went something like this:

Older swimmer: "So, what event are you swimming?"

Younger swimmer: "I don't know."

Older swimmer: "It's the breaststroke."

Younger swimmer: "Oh! Right! The breaststroke!"

Older swimmer: "So what do your hands do for the breaststroke turn?"

Younger swimmer: "I don't know."

Older swimmer: "The two-hand touch."

Younger swimmer: "Oh! Right! The two-hand touch!"

The breaststroke and butterfly strokes require a symmetrical two-hand touch on the wall. Forgetting that detail would disqualify the swimmer. So just by having this last-minute review, our youngest swimmers improved. No more DQs because of forgetting a critical detail or swimming the wrong stroke.

We saw the older swimmers hug the younger swimmers and say, "Good swim!" no matter who won or lost. It was really sweet to watch.

We never expected what happened next.

When it was time for the older swimmers to line up, their younger buddies went over to stand with them in line; they wanted to be helpful and imitate their older buddies. This was the conversation that started happening:

Younger swimmer: "So, what event is this?"

Older swimmer (feeling kind of silly): "Um, it's the breaststroke."

Younger swimmer: "Very good! What about the breast-stroke touch?"

Older swimmer (finally getting it): "Yes, the two-hand touch!"

Younger swimmer: "Very good, the two-hand touch!"

It was so adorable! And at the end of the older buddies' races, the younger buddies were there with the towels and hugs, saying, "Very good swim!"

Just that one idea made such a difference for our team—not only at meets, but also at practices.

Older swimmers started acting more responsibly, because they knew they were role models for the younger swimmers. Younger swimmers wanted to impress the older swimmers, so their behavior improved as well. And having a personal cheerleader helped everyone's attitude.

In fact, older teammates started watching their younger partners more carefully and began to give them pointers. "Don't hold your hand like that. Do it like this. Kick this way, not that way."

All the swimmers were more committed to showing up at practice, because someone else was counting on them.

In fact, when swimmers didn't come to practice, it wasn't unusual for buddies to go to their homes to find out why. We didn't ask anyone to do this; it just happened.

Suddenly, besides me and the assistant coaches, the older half of the team took on the role of personal coaches for their younger buddies. They started really caring about one another; they were becoming a team.

Lesson 1: Good teamwork comes from both buddies and coaches.

The second observation was that it wasn't always fun to be on the swim team. Let's face it: most kids were on the team because their parents forced them to join. **It was boring, and it was hard work—all those skills and drills.** We had practice every morning, Tuesday through Friday, and every evening, Tuesday through Thursday.

They suggested that we do skills and drills only in the mornings. The evening practices would be a series of games and fun activities in the water, designed to build strength and endurance.

Less boring practices led to better attendance and stronger swimmers.

The most fun I had with the assistant coaches was dreaming up these silly games for the team to play. I remember "kill the coach," during which all the assistant coaches had to walk back and forth on the edge of the pool, and the swimmers were treading water in the deep end, tossing large beach balls around, trying to hit one of the coaches. If they hit one of us, we had to dramatically "die," grasping for breath, clutching the site of our "wound," and flopping into the water.

They also suggested finding a way to create more fun at the actual swim meets. **They decided that we needed a ritual to pump us up and that we needed a stronger team identity.**

Our team was called the Maxwell SeaHawks. I created a huge banner for home meets and a smaller travel banner for away meets. I bought a stuffed animal—a hawk—and sewed a Maxwell SeaHawks patch on its chest. I attached it to the end of a long pole. Every time we had a meet, I would find and buy a mascot to represent the other team—and sew its mascot in the talons of our SeaHawk! The team would march around the pool, holding the pole high, so everyone could see the SeaHawk with a stingray or a dolphin or an alligator in its talons. At away meets, we would take some of the water from our pool and pour it into the other team's pool, as if to "infect" their pool with our essence.

Eventually, we started writing cheers, which were chanted like cadence chants for military marching. The ones who wrote the cheer would chant out each line to be repeated by the rest of the team. Before we drove to any meet, pads of paper and pencils were given to all the cars, and swimmers and parents collaborated on the words to our cheers. I wish I had kept copies; some of them were so funny. I remember only one; Ben Weber, wherever you are, I know you enjoyed this one as much as we did:

I don't know but I've been told . . .

I don't know but I've been told . . .

Selma's coach is getting old . . .

Selma's coach is getting old . . .

Every practice, Ben is there . . .

Every practice, Ben is there . . .

Watching from his rocking chair . . .

Watching from his rocking chair . . .

Ben Weber was the coach of the Selma Gators, and he wasn't much older than I was! He was so much fun, we decided to make him a traveling banner as a present.

The following year, almost every team started doing cheers before the meets! Everyone had strange rituals! The Selma Gators actually gave the Maxwell SeaHawks a pair of real, live chickens, calling us the Maxwell chickens! (Who won that meet? We tied!) We gave the chickens to the Montgomery Zoo, and our swim team made the local paper!

Lesson 2: A group of diverse people will generate creative ideas and improve learning.

The third observation was that, even though everyone did the same practices together, those practices didn't take into account all the swimmers' individual needs and talents.

So we started breaking out into clinics during the skills-and-drills mornings. We needed the different assistant coaches to lead different parts of the practice. If you needed to work on your flip turns but not your dives, then you would spend more time on flip turns and skip diving practice.

This meant that assistant coaches would be giving up their own practice time. That wasn't a good thing, because they were still competing in the meets. I suggested they swim with me before practice. I used to swim a mile before each practice, every morning, and every evening. They thought that was a great idea.

Even better was this: the swimmers, who were now seldom late because swim practice had become much more fun, started noticing that the assistant coaches and I were doing laps before practice.

They were amazed that we still worked on our own skills and drills, even though we were the coaches. It sent a good message to them and to their parents, who commented that they had never seen the previous coach even get into the water.

Lesson 3: Integrity builds trust and models authenticity.

The fourth observation was that the whole business just felt too competitive. There were the stars who always seemed to win races—and the rest of the team, who didn't. The suggestion was to change the focus.

Rather than making a big deal about who won which race, why not make a big deal about each swimmer's personal best time?

I knew this was a great idea, because it was exactly what kept me on the swim team in college. If I compared myself to the other swimmers in the pool, meet after meet, I would be a loser, loser, loser. But I knew that each time I swam in a race, that particular race was the best race of my life! So, meet after meet, I was a winner, winner, winner. I always beat my previous best time.

So that was the next change. Older buddies hardly mentioned how their younger buddies placed—as in, "Good Job! Third place!" Instead, it was, "Awesome! You swam three seconds faster than last time!"

Because they practiced all week and became stronger, every swimmer improved with each meet. With the old focus, we had one winner and seven losers. **With our new focus, every single swimmer was a winner, every race!**

Even our swim team banquet at the end of the season changed its focus. No more awards based on how fast anyone swam or how many points they earned at meets.

The awards were given to emphasize the personalities of the swimmers or funny things that had happened.

For example, one year, there were three girls on the team named Jennifer. Each Jennifer received the Most Common Name on the Swim Team Award. One of them was Jennifer Pool. She also received the Best Name on the Swim Team Award. Parents found the banquet as entertaining as the swimmers did. **They loved hearing the stories and laughing at the awards we created.**

One year, we had a swimmer who actually missed every single swim meet! He received the Marinara Award. Why? Because marinara sauce is tomato sauce with "no meet."

That season was really great. We had more fun together, the team doubled in size because families were finding out how much the kids enjoyed it, and we finally had a winning record. **We actually won a few more meets than we lost.**

The following season was actually easier, because the assistant coaches really knew what they were doing. Halfway through the summer, we still hadn't lost a meet! We began to wonder, "Now that we are getting really good, should we change our method? Do something different? Look more closely at our opponents? Use more deliberate strategy when placing swimmers in events, one based on our times and the times of our opponents? Maybe we should use this new competitive edge to our advantage."

Maybe we should really try to craft a
championship team.
Nope!
We decided not to.
We were having too much fun being a
noncompetitive team.

Everyone's times were improving, the team members enjoyed one another, parents were happy, and honestly, we just didn't care about the score at the end of the meet. Well, we cared, but not enough to change our focus. In other words, if we suddenly became too stressed out about winning, we might lose what we had worked so hard to create.

So we decided to keep our official noncompetitive focus. **We would stick with our main goals of having fun, improving skills, and learning teamwork.** It was then that I truly realized that every single assistant coach was on the same page. They all wanted the same thing. That was hugely important, because if just one of the assistant coaches really wanted to make things more competitive, we would be pulling the team in different directions, and everything would have broken down.

Lesson 4: Shared goals are needed to move the group in the right direction.

Well, we kept on winning. In fact, we went all the way; we were undefeated, and we won the division championship. It was 1985. What a meet! What an amazing two seasons! We stopped obsessing about winning meets and started winning more meets! **We deliberately became less competitive, and we competed better!**

But more than that championship meet, I remember that team and those assistant coaches. I remember their honesty and wisdom, their excitement about teaching the rest of the team, their dedication to improving as a leadership team, and the way they cared about one another.

I couldn't have built up that team on my own. If I wanted to create a terrific swim team, I would need the wisdom and ideas and feedback of the folks who were actually on the swim team. They were the experts. They were the ones who modeled leadership skills in a way that compelled the younger swimmers to imitate them.

And why doesn't that happen more often?

Why doesn't the bank president ask for feedback from the person who mops the floor and cleans the toilets?

Why doesn't the restaurant owner invite ideas from the folks who cook, serve meals, and bus tables? I am certain that "ordinary" workers have wisdom that bank presidents and restaurant owners need to listen to.

Lesson 5: Everyone has something to offer; everyone has something to learn.

I am telling you this story because I want you to know how much I believe in the wisdom of young people. How did I learn this? From listening to young people! They taught me in 1985. They taught me again in 2002.

So don't take my word for it! **Who am I, anyway? Some lady who's dying!** Someone you'll never even met. So if you have no reason to believe me, believe the Alabama teenagers who turned a swim team around and made them champions in just two years. Or believe the Wisconsin teenagers who taught forty-five workshops and created five leadership training videos in three years. Take their advice. If you do, I know you will transform your friends, your school, your workplace, your community, and even yourself.

Dream big.
Learn humbly.
Reflect honestly.
Lead bravely.
Serve graciously.
Support tenderly.
Transform much.

8

Life Is Not Easy—So Forgive

Life is full of disappointments.

- You don't get the grade you think you deserved on a project you worked really hard on, yet some other student whose project was half as good as yours gets a better grade.

- Your boyfriend or girlfriend breaks up with you, and you really thought she/he was "the one."

- You get fired from your job for no good reason, and you needed the money to pay for a trip or Christmas presents or something else very important.

- Your friend tells a secret he or she promised not to tell, and you decide that moving away, dying your hair, and changing your name is your only option for avoiding lifelong embarrassment.

The Tale of Two Sisters

I remember hearing a heartbreaking story from one of my friends. Daisy has two cousins—twins—who haven't spoken to each other in more than five years. Nicole and Natalie were close growing up. They weren't identical twins; in fact, Nicole was more attractive, more athletic, and even smarter. It was actually kind of embarrassing for Natalie as a child. People often said things like, "You two are twins? You don't even look like sisters."

She heard the whisperings, "Too bad Natalie didn't turn out more like Nicole."

They never knew their dad; they lived with their single mom. **Natalie always felt that Nicole was the favored one.** And why not? Nicole was a varsity athlete, straight-A student, and always had a boyfriend. Nicole had no boyfriends, hated sports, and earned more Cs than Bs.

Nicole went to college, went to pharmacy school, got married, and had several gorgeous children.

Their mom developed muscular sclerosis and needed constant help, so Natalie stayed home and took care of her. She had a part-time job with very flexible hours, so she didn't mind. She knew Nicole had her hands full with her young family.

When their mom died, she left her house and much more money to Natalie. Nicole was outraged. Even though Natalie became the favored daughter by staying home and giving up everything to take care of their mom, Nicole still expected their mother to be fair and give them an equal amount of money. She couldn't help thinking that Natalie had somehow manipulated the situation.

My friend Daisy explained it to me. Their mom knew what she was doing; she made it clear to her brother, Daisy's dad. Natalie had no idea about her mother's will. But their mom knew that Nicole had everything going for her, with a husband, a great career, lots of money, and tons of friends. **Natalie had nothing—still no boyfriend, a job at a coffee shop, and her whole adult life had been spent taking care of her mother.** Her mother wanted her to have the money she needed to finally go to college and start to enjoy life. She had already paid for Nicole's college, grad school, and wedding. Why shouldn't Natalie get the same?

But according to Nicole, it was not "the same." Natalie got almost everything her mother had left.

Daisy's whole family is still broken up about this. Neither of the twins will come to any family gatherings, for fear that the other twin will show up.

They have missed Thanksgiving dinners, Christmas parties, weddings, baptisms, even funerals—for five years.

Both sisters feel as if the other one was the "favored" one, and neither can forgive her twin for what has happened.

Daisy asked me for advice. What could she do? I couldn't think of anything that might help at this point. If they won't even show up for a family funeral, then they might be beyond anyone's influence.

> All I could tell her was the little bit I know about forgiveness.

Forgiveness for an Imperfect World

Life is not easy, and sometimes people get hurt. Whenever there is a rift in a relationship, the harm will continue to get worse until it's addressed. It's like carrying around a backpack and stuffing all your anger and bitterness into it. After five years of that, you're going to develop all kinds of back pain, shoulder pain, and other problems.

In a perfect world, a complete reconciliation could take place. Nicole and Natalie might both spontaneously decide that they love Aunt Tillie so much they just couldn't stay away from her funeral. So as they miraculously enter the church at the same time, in front of the whole family, with the steeple bells ringing, they burst into tears and a loving chorus of "I'm so sorry. Won't you please forgive me?" And sisters, cousins, and the entire family tree live happily ever after.

But you know the world's not perfect.

Daisy thinks it's Nicole's fault for getting so angry about their mother's will. But Natalie's lifelong envy of her sister's good looks (and good luck) made it easy to play the martyr's role.

So let's start with Nicole. She said some terrible things about Natalie when the whole thing started, especially the possible implication that Natalie might have tried to manipulate her mother's will. If Nicole doesn't apologize and repent, she will remain imprisoned in denial. She will continue to live without any understanding for Natalie and her situation. **In fact, it might affect her overall ability to have compassion for *anyone*.** She will never truly be at peace, and she won't be able to move forward with her life in a healthy way.

Nicole's backpack is just too heavy. It's weighing her down.

Keeping all that anger and bitterness inside is only hurting her. It's like a prison without any bars. She's choosing to stay trapped; she cannot move.

Meanwhile, if Natalie doesn't forgive Nicole, she is also imprisoned by the past. **Her anger and bitterness will also become destructive.** She'll be stuffing it all into her backpack as well, feeling the pain and choosing the prison. She won't really be able to move forward with her life in a healthy way, either.

However, even if Nicole never apologizes and never repents, Natalie can still escape her prison. Regardless of what Nicole decides to do, Natalie can still forgive Nicole. She can open her backpack, admit her role in making things worse, and let go of all that anger and bitterness. She can stop resenting how Nicole had the perfect life growing up and has the perfect family now.

That doesn't mean that what Nicole said and did was OK. It just means that Natalie will put an end to how this resentment has been destroying her life all these years. **By forgiving Nicole, Natalie will have new freedom.** Her backpack can be emptied out, and she will be able to move forward again. She can reconnect with all the family members who love her and have missed her for five years. Natalie's refusal to forgive wasn't really hurting Nicole; it was hurting Natalie. She was only hurting herself all along.

And even if Natalie never forgives her, Nicole can still escape her prison. Regardless of what Natalie decides to do, Nicole can still apologize. She can write a letter, send an e-mail, make a phone call. *She can repent.* She can also open her backpack and let go of all that anger and bitterness. She can stop resenting all the money their mom gave to Natalie. After all, she and her husband are very fortunate and living comfortably.

Even if Natalie still refuses to speak with Nicole, refuses to accept her apology, and refuses to forgive her, Nicole can forgive herself for her selfish words and actions. By doing that, Nicole will have new freedom. Her backpack will be emptied out, and she will be able to move forward again. She can reconnect with all the family members who love her and have missed her for five years. Nicole's refusal to apologize wasn't really hurting Natalie; it was hurting Nicole. She was only hurting herself all along.

Complete reconciliation would require repentance and forgiveness from both sisters.

But even without complete reconciliation, either or both women can find peace.

The point is this: we can't always have a complete reconciliation. We can control only what we ourselves do. But even if the other person refuses to be part of the process, we can always repent. **We can always forgive.**

Repentance and forgiveness will always bring us freedom and peace.

Take Nicole and Natalie—add up their years of anger; add some outrage; sprinkle in some prejudice, racism, and hatred; and you will begin to understand why countries go to war. Anger and hatred for our enemies can become more important to us than the lives of our own sons and daughters. We have to start loving everyone's sons and daughters more than we hate our perceived enemies.

And Now, a Tale of Two Brothers

I wish Nicole and Natalie could have met Ethan and Austin—not twins, but brothers, only two years apart. Maybe hearing this brotherly story would have helped Nicole and Natalie envision forgiveness between siblings.

Ethan and Austin were normal, healthy, and competitive brothers. They shared a room, so there were plenty of arguments just about their living space. One was too cold, the other too hot. One was too messy, the other too picky. One was always "stealing" clothes from the other one.

Julie, their mom, often got tired of nagging and begging them to quit fighting. One year, she told me that she was making a New Year's resolution about less nagging.

But just a few days later, everything went wrong.

Ethan was still home from college on Christmas break, and Julie wanted the rest of vacation to go smoothly. On this particular Sunday morning, she noticed two things right away. First, the car keys were not hung up on the kitchen hook. Did she nag? Nope. She didn't say a word. She also noticed that the new cordless phone was not hung up on its cradle. Did she nag? Nope. *These things will just have to get worked out on their own,* she thought.

Austin went to church that morning with his mom and dad, but Ethan had to go to work; he had a seasonal job at a local restaurant.

After church, they walked into their house, and Austin picked up a piece of paper from the floor. He shoved it at his dad and ran into the kitchen to pick up the phone. "It's not working," he reported as he ran upstairs to check the other phones.

Julie asked, "What's going on?" "This note from Ethan," explained her husband, Mark. "It says, 'No car keys, phone dead, will try to catch a bus to work.'"

"Catch a bus? Has he ever taken a city bus before? How does he know which buses run where and when?" Julie couldn't understand what Ethan was thinking.

Mark shrugged. "He doesn't have a clue. Ethan left for college right before we moved here. He never took a bus anyplace. He doesn't know his way around the city. I can't imagine what he did."

Julie was so angry, she wanted to kick herself. She felt totally responsible. If only she hadn't decided to stop nagging. "Keys missing? Phone went dead? I'll never make another New Year's resolution again."

Austin emerged from the stairway, looking guilty and sheepish.

"It's all my fault," he volunteered.

"I had the keys in my pocket all morning. I forgot to hang them up last night. And I never turned the new phone off. I should have just hung it up on the wall, like I'm supposed to. The phone's not dead. It was just off the hook." (This was back in the days when cordless phones were new and you had to keep them in the cradle or the line was disconnected.)

He collapsed into a chair, disgusted with himself. "I think I'll call Ethan and apologize. I could pay him back for the bus fare and for the pay he missed out on. I wonder how late he was."

His dad handed him the phone. Austin called the restaurant and asked for Ethan.

Austin's side of the conversation sounded like this:

Oh, Ethan, I'm so sorry.
Oh, no.
Oh, I'm so sorry.
Really?
OH, NO.
I'm so sorry, Ethan.
I'm really so sorry.

This seemed to go on for ten minutes. After he hung up, he told his parents the details.

Ethan asked folks at the bus stop for information. Some-one told him which bus to take, but then he had to wait twenty minutes before it came. Then it took almost an hour before he arrived at work. He was an hour and a half late. They put him on notice, which meant one more slipup and he would be fired. He probably could have walked there faster.

Austin felt sick over this. He knew money could never make it up to his brother.

Julie just kept thinking, *See what happens when parents don't nag? I should have asked about the keys. I should have told someone to find the phone and hang it up. When Ethan comes home, there's going to be a huge fight. I don't blame him.*

Julie waited all day for Ethan to come home and murder his brother.

It never happened. By the time Mark picked Ethan up and brought him home, he was already quite calm. Austin greeted him at the door whimpering, ***"I'm so sorry, Ethan. It was all my fault. I'm so sorry."***

But here was Ethan's response. "I was really mad earlier today, but I'm just not mad anymore. I know you didn't do it on purpose. I forget things, too. I could have been the one to leave the keys in my coat pocket. If I stay mad at you, I only hurt myself. It's over, and it can't be undone. So why sulk and stay mad? **Let's just forget about it.**"

Julie was amazed. "What did you say to him in the car?" she asked her husband.

"Not a thing. He was already fine." Mark was just as surprised.

Julie called me the next day to tell me this story. She said, "When did Ethan grow up and become so reasonable? What happened to the two brothers who used to beat each other up until blood and tears were flowing freely? How could he forgive so easily? Where did he learn that?"

I reminded her that they had two good parents at home who did lots of good modeling.

She told me she secretly keeps thinking about what her own response would have been, "If I'd had to take a bus and be late because of his actions, he'd be grounded for two weeks." She also concluded, "To heck with the no-nagging policy." She said she still has a lot to learn about patience—and forgiveness. I told her that this time she had the honor of learning from her children. I could hear her emotional response on the phone—I think she was trying to choke back some tears.

Forgiveness Strategies

I was interviewed about a year ago on a radio show. The person asked me what I thought my most important talent or gift was. She probably expected me to talk about my writing or my teaching. I surprised both of us with my answer.

> I could hardly believe it when I heard myself say, "I think I'm really good at forgiving."

It turned the whole conversation around. I don't know where that came from. But ever since then, I have realized that not only is it true but also it has really been a focal point of my life.

I have had my share of sadness and disappointment. **You don't live over fifty years without getting your heart broken—several times.** For the really horrible, awful, "How could he do this to me?" kind of outrage and grief, my strategy is easy.

- **Step 1: I cry a lot.** Sometimes I do it while listening to music or watching mindless television. Sometimes I eat junk food. This could last a day, a week, or once in a while, even longer. (I'm too embarrassed to tell you how long it has lasted.)

- **Step 2: I mentally fast-forward to some point of time in the future.** I picture the person who did me wrong. I craft my own ending to the story. I picture this person, perhaps years from now, doubled over in agony, regretting his decision. I imagine him saying, "How could I have been so foolish? Why was I so cruel to such a gorgeous, brilliant, amazing woman? I will never forgive myself." Sometimes I even imagine that I have died before he has this fantastic insight. And it doesn't take me long to start feeling sorry for the poor guy. After all, I'm so gorgeous, brilliant, and amazing. See what he left behind? No wonder he is beside himself with grief.

Sometimes I write a poem about it. Sometimes I write a short story about it. But the greatest part of all this is that, somehow, it becomes so easy for me to feel compassion for the person who wronged me that it also becomes easy for me to forgive him for hurting me.

I get too tired from all the energy it takes to stay angry. It's the forgiveness that brings me peace.

That second step is really awesome. It doesn't work merely for romantic heartaches; it works just as well for ridiculous inconveniences, such as a driver tailgating me and then speeding off at about twenty miles over the speed limit. In my fantasy world, I conjure up all kinds of reasons a driver might do that. Maybe she's having a baby. Maybe his wife is having a baby. Maybe his mistress is having a baby. Maybe his pregnant mistress is on her way to tell his wife who the daddy is. And before you know it, I'm laughing at my own silliness.

I have done this with my own kids, my friends, and my family. It's infectious. Once I begin the ridiculous scenarios, they can listen only so long before they start chiming in, adding their own ideas. In no time, we are amusing ourselves with our own creativity. It doesn't matter that none of our ideas is true; it makes no difference whether the person we're talking about is completely in the wrong. **If there's nothing we can do about it, why stay angry? The anger only hurts *us*.** It's always more fun to have fun and laugh.

It works in traffic jams, in long lines at the bank or the movies, on hold during ridiculous business phone calls—you name it. Don't bother getting mad. Just get funny and creative. You'll find yourself forgiving every major and minor mishap of your day, and you'll come home much happier.

How Much Pain Is Anger Worth?

You might wonder whether step 2 can really work all the time. After all, some pretty big disasters happen out there.

Aren't some situations simply unforgivable?

I guess that's up to you. Are some situations so horrible that it's worth stuffing all that anger, resentment, bitterness, and rage into your backpack so you have to drag it around the rest of your life until it's so heavy you can't move at all, and you have created an invisible prison for yourself?

Remember, your forgiveness doesn't mean that what the other person did was OK.

Remember also that if you insist on staying angry, it doesn't affect that other person at all. (Most of the time, that person you are angry at doesn't even know the difference.) **Your forgiveness affects only you.**

Forgiveness means not holding grudges against people, letting go of past hurts and arguments, letting go of jealousy and envy, being content with the way things are when you cannot have your own way, and even "praying for your enemies."

Easier said than done, I know.

So what if someone rapes you?
What if someone rapes your sister or your
girlfriend?
What if someone kills your brother, or your mother,
or your best friend, or your husband?
What if some people come up with a horrific plan
and crash three airplanes into buildings,
killing thousands of innocent people?

No, in situations like that, silly stories aren't enough.

When those kinds of things happen, step 1—the crying and grieving and feeling—can take a year or two—or ten. Step 2 sometimes involves some kind of professional counseling. Sometimes it involves even the criminal justice system. Sometimes it involves spiritual direction. But when it results in forgiveness—and it always can—there is healing, relief, freedom, and peace.

I wish I could protect you from anyone who
might hurt you.
But I can't.
Life is too brutal.
There is no way to avoid suffering.

Learning how to forgive is one of the most essential tasks of adulthood.

It's a daunting skill to acquire. But I do promise you this: the more you forgive, even in small ways, the easier and less painful it becomes. Then some day, when you are faced with an unspeakable tragedy, you may be up to the impossible task of forgiveness.

9

Respect Time and Cherish Memories

When I was first learning to cook, one of the most creative meals my mom taught me was meat loaf. Such a simple basic foundation: chopped meat, a couple of raw eggs to hold it together, bread crumbs, and whatever else you want. You rolled it up into a ball, or shaped it to fit into one of those meat-loaf pans, and cooked it at 350 degrees for an hour or so.

At first, I would add just a handful of spices—maybe basil, oregano, onion, and garlic—and some tomato sauce. (Ground-turkey meat loaf would often get maybe parsley, sage, rosemary, thyme, and some mushroom soup.) But after a while, my brother Steve started helping me, and we'd get braver and start adding other things: chopped olives, onions, celery, tomato, mushrooms, peppers—basically, whatever we had in the fridge. Sometimes we'd use oatmeal instead of bread crumbs. Sometimes we'd use rice. Sometimes we'd use celery soup or cheddar-cheese soup.

We never made the same meat loaf twice.

Dad would come home and sniff the air and ask, "Have Lisa and Steve been experimenting with meat loaf again?" He'd try but could seldom guess our ingredients.

But whatever we put into it, the next day, the meat-loaf sandwiches were even better. My mom would remind us that the spices had grown stronger. Dad would say, "Variety is the spice of life," and Mom would say memories were like that. **Just as spices grow stronger over time, so do our most significant memories.**

Memories as Real Treasure

Around the time I was learning to cook, **I kept a memory box**—about the size of a shoebox—which I decorated and used to keep special items. I'd go through it every so often and clear out the items whose significance I could no longer remember.

But by the time I finished college, I had so much stuff that I had graduated from a simple memory box to an entire footlocker.

One of the first things I did with my sons after my cancer diagnosis was go through my foot locker and show them all my scrapbooks and special items.

I had one of my dad's stethoscopes, my mom's gavel from when she was president of a leadership club, and other significant items. We spent a weekend just telling the stories about the contents in that locker. I was amazed that they were so interested. They said they learned more about me during our "reflection weekend" than they had all their years put together.

When my parents were getting close to their twenty-fifth wedding anniversary, my brothers and I talked about how to make it special. **Our parents did not want a party, and they hated surprises.** We decided to create a twenty-fifth-anniversary scrapbook. We contacted all our close friends and family, and we sent each of them a fancy page from a fancy scrapbook. We asked them to create a page of memories—photographs, drawings, stories, whatever they wanted—to make the anniversary special for my parents.

We got so much more than we asked for. Many sent old photos and told stories my parents had long forgotten. Some glued special items to their page; some attached cards or notes that my parents had sent to them.

When we presented them with this giant collection of memories, they didn't take their eyes off the book for maybe forty-eight hours.

I'm not sure they ever went to sleep. It was an incredible reflection of their entire engaged and married life, as seen through the eyes of their loved ones. We kids loved it, too. It answered a lot of questions regarding who was whose friend, who met whom, and when and where, and so on.

I had hoped to do the same thing for their fiftieth wedding anniversary, but never did. There was never even a thirtieth anniversary. Just a few years later, my dad died suddenly, from a heart attack. We never had a chance to say good-bye. We were all in shock. He was healthy, he exercised and watched his weight, seemed to be the kind of man who would live into his hundreds. He was more alive than the next ten people you might know. Full of stories, full of fun, a walking party wherever he went.

He was a physician and a surgeon, and he was so funny and charming that his patients truly adored him. He relied on his own concoction of broken Sicilian dialect (learned during childhood from his grandparents) when he couldn't think of the right word while trying to communicate with his Spanish-speaking patients. At his funeral, a gentle man approached me and said, "I mopped the third floor of the hospital, where your dad did most of his surgery."

"He was the only doctor who called me by name. Every morning. I'll never forget him."

My three brothers and I are lucky enough to be a tiny bit like him in some way. When people think we're funny or creative, or insightful or clever, we just look at one another and think, *This is nothing. Too bad you never got to meet our dad. I am nothing but a shadow compared to what this man was.* He died in 1983, but it still seems like last week.

Several years later, on the tenth anniversary of his death, I was at a conference. Instead of going out to eat with my colleagues, I stayed alone in my hotel room with an idea. I thought about my dad and started listing some of his favorite sayings, his favorite stories, and some of my favorite memories about him. When I got home, I sent my list to my brothers to get them thinking. The next time we got together, we expanded the stories and added some details. The result was fifteen or twenty pages of stories, favorite phrases, general descriptions, and memories.

Then I took some highlights, sent a few samples to all our family and family friends, and said, "Please contact me and tell us your favorite stories about our dad. Here are just a few memory starters we came up with."

In no time, I had an amazing collection of stories and memories. Sometimes two different relatives wrote about the same story, and the details were completely different. No problem. I didn't try to establish the "historical" truth. I just put in one story, then wrote, "Cousin so-and-so remembered this same story somewhat differently," and then added the other version.

Most often, each story had a point. We didn't ask for this "commentary," but most people ended their story with a statement about my dad ("This shows how caring he was" or "He was a leader; he had his own style" Or "He was brilliant and delightfully funny"). I realized that the purpose for each friend or family member was not only to tell me a story but also to teach me something important about my dad. The details of the story were less important than the teaching. **And every story taught us this: "You had a remarkable dad. We loved him so."**

I typed them all up, made copies, and put them into binders. That was our Christmas gift to my mom and to every family member that year. I bet we made thirty or more binders. Every few pages we included family photos as well.

Every year on the anniversary of my dad's death, wherever I am, I read the entire binder, start to finish.

And when anyone remembered additional stories, we wrote them up, and added them in, at the end of our binders.

That group reflection of my dad, with contributions made from several loved ones who are also no longer alive, has brought me great comfort over the years.

How We Have Loved Others through Memories

Life is filled with the unexpected. We were actually worried about my mom dying young (she had been diagnosed with breast cancer when I was in college), and yet the Christmas we thought might be her last ended up being my dad's last one.

My mom ended up living more years as a widow than as a wife. She never lost her devotion and affection to my dad. I would call her on every day of significance—his birthday, the day of his death, their anniversary—and I'd never need to mention it. She'd say, "I knew you would call me today." It was our little way of remembering. Usually, there was a good story or two shared with every one of those phone calls.

When my mom's cancer came back, they told her she might live another five to ten years. They were right; she lived for seven more years. I came to visit her on Valentine's Day weekend of 2009. She shared a home with my oldest brother, Joe; his wife, Heidi; and their two daughters, Bernadette and Barbara. My youngest brother, David, and his wife, Rosemary, lived only twenty minutes away, so we tended to have frequent family gatherings. My middle brother, Steve; his wife, Marie; and their daughter, Elizabeth, lived only four hours away in Massachusetts. When the three cousins were much younger, we made more trips out to see the Massachusetts Calderones. As the girls got older, it was the Massachusetts Calderones who came down to visit New Jersey more often.

Every long weekend I came to visit, there would always be some cooking or craft project I planned to do with my nieces, often related to the season or holiday: cookies, cupcakes, or Chex Mix (or meat loaf) and all kinds of plastic, foam rubber, fabric, wood, or needle crafts.

But on Valentine's Day weekend in 2009, Friday night, my mom had special plans for me.

She said, "Tomorrow is *my* day. Remember?" She had asked me to go through all her favorite knickknacks with her and make a list of which friend or family member was to get which one, and I was to take notes about each item, write each person a letter, and gift wrap them.

However, that next day, she woke up and didn't seem to know our names. She had completely forgotten what day it was and how to get dressed. She stared at us with fear and confusion. We never got to do the project we had been looking forward to doing. (After her death, my sister-in-law Heidi and I went through her things and guessed at who might be the most appropriate person to receive this or that item. I wrote the notes, but they were based on our own guesses and observations, not my mom's.)

After that Valentine's Day, my mom began living in room 302 of Peggy House. This was not a complete shock to us. **Mom had been living with cancer, getting chemotherapy, getting radiation, living by a giant calendar and schedule of pills for years.** If you saw her socially, you would probably never even guess that she had tumors growing in her bones (and later in her brain). It was a very slow process, and she was dealing with each gradual change. That's probably why she had postponed her knickknack project until that February weekend; she thought she had so much more time.

Once she was in the hospice, even though I lived in Milwaukee, I was determined to come visit her for a week every month. And mostly, I did that.

However, the diagnosis of my own cancer a few months later made everything a little more complicated for our whole family.

We never did tell my mom about it. She probably would not have understood. And if she had understood, it would have broken her heart.

Much of the time, she didn't remember our names. I'd always greet her with, "Hi, Mom. It's me, your daughter Lisa." and she'd smile and say, "Of course." But if one of the nurses had asked her, "Who is this woman?" I'm sure she wouldn't be able to say my name on many days. **Yet it seemed as if she at least recognized that we loved her, and we were "with her," so she usually trusted us when she saw us.**

I had given her a Christmas present just two months before she moved to Peggy House.

It was a little booklet called "Lessons from Mom."

It was a set of thirteen different lessons she had taught me over the years, and how I had applied some of those lessons to my life, and what the positive results had been, with little pictures illustrating the lessons.

I am certain she never read it. I found it still in the same box I wrapped it in. So I started bringing it to Peggy House with me. Every day, I read her a story or two. She loved hearing the stories of what she taught me and how they benefited me in my life. She would look at me and say, "I said that?" I got to assure her every day, "Yes, you did, Mom. You were always so smart and so willing to teach me important things." She would just beam. And I could read the same stories over and over, because she never remembered hearing them before.

Keeping a memory box, making a scrapbook of photographs and cards to celebrate an anniversary or birthday, asking friends and loved ones to remember stories after someone has died, putting together a list of lessons you learned from someone special—these are some of the best ways we have preserved the most precious reflections of our families and friends.

Personal reflections, private thoughts,
shared memories, public stories—
they are so essential to who we are
and what it means to belong to a family
or an intentional group of friends.

All it takes is time to bring them together and let their meaning teach us.

Make Your Time Count

When you are young, it's so easy to assume you will have more than enough time to do these kinds of things. And usually, that's the case.

But time is fleeting. We never know what will happen on any given day.

So make your time count.

Mark special days such as birthdays and anniversaries with deliberate memories. Take time to write something significant on index cards or fancy paper and wrap them up. Simple things such as, "I remember when . . ." or "I love how you . . ." or "One of the most fun times I've had with you was . . ." or "Thank you for . . ." These are the gifts that will be treasured over the years.

Mark the not-so-special days by just being present. **Don't waste time staying angry or letting someone else stew in the hurt that you created by a nasty remark or thoughtless comment.**

Mark your good-byes, even the daily ones. Hug your parents good-bye. Learn to say, **"I love you."** Hug your siblings, give them the side-by-side half hug, or at least take five seconds to look them in the eye and say, "Have a fun day," or "I'll think of you today," or "Make today count." **Don't blow it off.** *Make it count.*

Imagine this:

What if that moment, before you all shuffle off
to school or work is the last moment you ever
see one of your parents or siblings again?
Or it ends up being the last memory they have
of you?
What do you want that very last phrase or
gesture or communication to be?

I guarantee this: if it's the last one, that memory will grow
stronger and more powerful over the years, just like the
spices in a meat loaf. If it was loving and positive, you
will be forever grateful you took that moment and made
it count.

10

Live a Reflected-Upon Life

Lots of people live very busy lives. I know I did. Every week I had meetings, classes, and training sessions for which I made presentations. I also spent hours writing: articles, outlines and handouts for those meetings and classes and training sessions, grant proposals to get money, and grant reports to explain what we did with the money. Every one of those tasks had a deadline. Missing a deadline could mean losing thousands of dollars for the youth leadership programming and the events I was coordinating.

But we can become so very busy,
that we don't even get the chance to slow down,
reflect,
and connect the dots of our lives.

When I had a "public" workday, I would get dressed up and drive around to maybe three events in one day. When I had a "stay-home" workday, I didn't even get out of my pajamas. I would start working at my computer around five or six in the morning, and I would not finish until sometimes ten at night. I could do two days' work in one. That's how I managed to juggle the responsibilities of what was actually two jobs: directing Tomorrow's Present, an inner-city youth leadership program I started, and finding all the money to keep it going. The money part meant budgets, bookkeeping, and reports; it also meant doing articles and workshops on the side to bring in money. When you start an organization, sometimes you have to do everything in the beginning, because you can barely raise enough money to cover your salary, program costs, and health insurance.

I could work such long hours because
(a) I loved what I was doing,
(b) I was good at what I was doing,
(c) I was working for a cause I truly believed in,
but most important,
(d) I made sure my schedule had time for
reflection and "off" time.

Why We Need to Reflect

I used to take off very long weekends (sometimes an entire week) to visit my family. When my mom moved to Peggy House, I kicked it up a notch. **When I took off that time, I could forget all about my job.** I was fully present for all that quality time with my family. That's when I was able to think, remember, and connect the dots. That was my major downtime, my reflection time, my time to renew whom I belonged to and to let the memories and meaning teach me.

Some people never do that. When they get away from school or their jobs, they go on some exciting, fast-paced vacation that still doesn't give them downtime. It doesn't give them rest time. It doesn't renew the meaning in their lives. They end up needing a vacation from their vacation.

Stressful life can drain us—it takes so much energy just to live!

Even when it's exciting and enjoyable, life doesn't naturally give us many empty places
and vacant hours
for us to reflect and fill back up.

We need that downtime for spiritual peace. We need it for our physical health, too.

I always got big chunks of it when I traveled to see my family. But I used to get little chunks of it in the swimming pool when I swam a mile three times a week. There I was all alone with nothing to see, hear, or smell except the water. I was completely alone with my thoughts.

Some great insights would pop into my head at those times. I would feel happy, content, blessed, aware, and calm. We need those moments—the little chunks of time as well as the big ones.

Otherwise, we don't get the chance to figure out who we are. Without that awareness, it's like driving along with no sense of direction. You might get there, you might not. If you do, you won't even know. You could have just missed the turn you wanted to make, or you might be lost forever.

We need time and reflection to figure out where we want to go. Without it, our life just seems aimless and pointless, and we end up doing all kinds of things we wish we hadn't. And we never figure out why.

It takes time to understand the meaning in our lives.

In order to take the time, we need to make reflection a priority.

How to Do It

You need to reflect deliberately, and it takes only a few basic steps, so basic, that many people do them without even knowing it. But just in case you're not doing it, I want you to start.

First, LIVE.

No kidding. **Really, just LIVE.** But don't live with your eyes closed. Live and notice. Pay attention. Be observant. Look around. Listen. Don't just go through the motions with your head down most of the time, all absorbed in your music or in texting and tweeting. Be part of LIFE. Interact with more than just electronic equipment.

Second, REVIEW your insights from life's lessons.

Do this deliberately—don't skip this part. You remember only the stuff you actually spend time thinking about. So, if you are a talker, talk with a trusted friend. If you are shy and quiet, write in your journal.

If you don't think you can do this on your own, find a support group; a book club; a group of friends who will be willing to do more than eat, drink, and watch sports or movies together. I used to hang with a group of teachers who had Friday-Night Prayer Meeting. Doesn't that make us all sound so holy? We all taught at Catholic schools. But Friday nights, we went out to a bar and talked all night. It was great. It was our time to talk and review our insights.

The point is this: *you must learn from life.* If you're not learning from life, you're not paying close enough attention. If your circle of friends aren't enough to help you really learn from life, then consider a mentor. It could be some trusted adult who is successful in some field you are interested in. You might also consider a professional counselor or a spiritual director. This is especially important if you are dealing with any issues of grief, anger, or trauma—issues that you haven't really resolved yet.

Third, take some QUIET TIME.

Really—quiet time is necessary, in big chunks and little chunks. It takes times for things to settle and to digest. So sit at a lake or ocean if you like that. Go for a walk. Go for a bike ride. Do yoga. Swim. Find some silent space where ideas and insights and decisions can catch your fancy. **Try praying or meditating.**

Nothing will bubble up to the surface unless there's some room. **So make room. Take time.** Make an appointment with yourself on your calendar to spend quiet time with the most important person in your life: YOU.

Fourth, RESOLVE your issues.

When you become aware of the changes inside of you: you become aware of the yearnings,
the passions,
the things that would bring you the fullness of life.

Then the really important, heroic, courageous stuff can happen: *you will begin to make all your decisions on the basis of this significant self-knowledge:*

- You might realize that you have a gift for music, and you feel empty when it's not part of your life. You don't want to leave your job and its steady income, but you might decide to give private music lessons or work with community theater.

- You might realize that you have a soft spot in your heart for animals, and you might start volunteering at an animal shelter.

- You might realize that you hate your major, you hate your job, and you want to do something that's a better match for who you really are. Then you take a leap of faith and try a different field—maybe you'll make the riskiest and best decision of your life.

- Or you realize that wasn't what you wanted after all. Either way, you will be learning about yourself. You will be living a reflective life. When you let reflection guide your life, it's always an adventure.

There are countless rewards for the person of reflection: most of all, peace of mind, a good night's sleep, and satisfaction when you look at yourself in the mirror every morning.

Once I was at a workshop on self-esteem. **The presenter told us, "One-third of the population is optimistic. One-third is kind of neutral. And one-third is actually pessimistic."** I was quite surprised at this information and gasped out loud. I turned to my neighbor and said, "How could that be possible? I'm sure there are more optimists than that." I didn't realize I had said it so loudly. The presenter chuckled and asked the group, "Guess which third she belongs to?"

It's Carpe Diem Day

One more thing about my parents, and how they died. **My father died too quickly.** We never got the chance to say good-bye. **My mother died too slowly.** We had so much time to say good-bye that we never really did it the way we wanted to. We kept postponing it, until she slipped into a lack of awareness—or into a new kind of awareness.

Not me. I seem to be the really lucky one. **I am dying at exactly the right speed—just fast enough for us to know it's urgent.** Just fast enough for my friends to say, "Whoa, we'd better celebrate with Lisa, because she might not be here in six months." And yet just slow enough for me to keep doing meaningful things for my loved ones.

For example, my mom never got the chance to go through her things and will them to people and help me write notes to them. But I've had time to do that with my things. For months, I had the joy of making lists and lists of dear friends and family, and going through all my things and deciding who would receive what.

Every item came with a love note, telling the person (let's say it's you) why I chose this item, how it reminds me of you, how it represents our relationship, and some of the things that make you so lovable to me, some of the things I want to thank you for, and some of the things I want you to remember about me.

What a delightful task. What a spectacular expression of love.

I had so much fun with this; it was a blessing to have a really good reason (my impending death) to honor people with a personal tribute. I cried with every love letter. I couldn't think of a better way to say good-bye. We had so many parties with my giveaways. The stories flowed, and the tears flowed, and the wine flowed, and our spirits soared. It seemed as if we were too happy to dwell on the sadness of my dying.

And yet below all the joy was this level of profound gratitude, this deep thankfulness that I had lived long enough to be blessed by so many loving friends and family members, and to have lived long enough to be able to see so many of them to tell them in person, in words, and in letters, with specific symbolic, personal items, of my deepest love, admiration, and affection.

And then, below all that happiness, below all that gratitude, there was indeed another layer—a layer of gripping sadness we could not deny.

There's the realization that life is too short, and when people we love pass away, we never quite recover.

In cancer circles, Carpe Diem Day is the anniversary of the day you were first told you had cancer. June 2 is my Carpe Diem Day.

It's meant to be a happy anniversary every year, a chance to say, "I lived one more year. I lived through four more seasons. I celebrated one more birthday. I am still alive."

I was given a six-month life expectancy.

I never expected to celebrate even one Carpe Diem Day.

But I got my chance. A few of my close friends, Sean and Peter (who now run Tomorrow's Present), took me out for dinner.

A few days later, I was on a plane to New Jersey. Peter was planning to visit me in New Jersey in two months. I thought I'd never see Sean again. It was a very difficult good-bye.

And then I flunked hospice and got shipped back to Milwaukee, until I was ready to take this dying thing seriously. No one expected me to live much longer than a few more months in Milwaukee.

When my second Carpe Diem Day came along, Sean and Pete were there to take me out again. This time, I had written a special song about it. I wrote it up on cards, gave them away, and asked people to sing it with me all night.

(You are probably too young to know the song, "Ta-ra-ra Boom-de-ay," but you can do a search and find it on YouTube. My Carpe Diem Day song is sung to the tune of "Ta-ra-ra Boom-de-ay."

It's Carpe Diem Day.
It's Carpe Diem Day.
Despite what doctors say,
I did not pass away.
Might not be here to stay.
But I am here today.
It's time to laugh and play
On Carpe Diem Day.

I truly do not expect to be alive for a third Carpe Diem Day.

That doesn't mean I don't have hope. I definitely have hope. **I have outrageous expectations.**

If I am not here on this planet, in this earthly life, that means I will be alive in the next life, and I know—I just know—that the miracles there will be beyond my wildest imagination.

And I have a pretty good imagination . . .

11

Go Ahead—Take the Plunge

I love swimming. I was on my college swim team, I coached a team in the 1980s, and I have continued to swim a mile three times a week for most of my adult life. I often got up at five or five-thirty in the morning to get a swimming start to my day.

Just a few months before they discovered my cancer, I started to feel faint in the locker room after my swim. I knew something was wrong. I'd feel so dizzy, I would sit on the shower floor to prevent myself from passing out. When my cancer was diagnosed, I wasn't even surprised.

After I had been through a few scans and procedures, whenever I could return to the pool, I always felt "normal" when I was back in the water. Maybe it was the only place where I didn't seem different. I hadn't told anyone at the YMCA pool yet, so mostly, they didn't know. Even with cancer, I was able to swim much faster than many of the senior citizens who did laps early in the morning in the lanes beside me.

Eventually, I could swim only half a mile at a time, then a third of a mile.

When I was living in New Jersey, my goal was to swim at least a quarter of a mile each time. After I finished, I was thoroughly exhausted. I went home and took a nap.

These days, I'm back in Milwaukee, and the folks at the local YMCA know all about my cancer. They know I have a do-not-resuscitate bracelet, and they worry when a week goes by and they don't see me. Now I swim only a few laps at a time, once or twice a week, before heading for the hot tub. **My belly is swollen with cancer growth, yet when I submerge myself in the water, it seems to be lifted up and supported.** It's the only time the pressure is relieved and my pain eases a bit.

The First Cold Shock

I have loved swimming my whole life, even when I was healthy and rode my bicycle to the pool on glorious summer mornings.

> When I first arrived at the pool,
> when I found myself at the water's edge,
> what do you think I did?
> The same thing I still do today.
> I hesitate.

Why? Why would I hesitate? Swimming is the thing I love to do. It's the thing I look forward to all week. It's the thing that brings me reflection time, me time; it brings spiritual insights. It's what keeps me sane. So why do I pause for even a moment?

I hesitate because I know what's coming.

The water is cold. I know that when I dive in, the shock of that cold will make me shiver for at least two laps until my heart gets pumping, and my blood gets moving, and my muscles get me going.

Does the fear of the shiver send me back to the locker room where I can safely get dressed and warm up and forget all this nonsense of cold water so early in the morning?

Of course not. I'm not saying that my knowledge of the cold changes my mind. I'm just saying that the knowledge of what's coming always causes me to hesitate.

All these years of swimming, each time I would hesitate but then realize that I couldn't procrastinate any longer. I would have to take the plunge. So I would dive in, get immediately jolted by the cold, emit a silent scream, and start swimming as fast as I could. My first two laps were painful. But then I started to warm up. By the third or fourth lap, I started to feel great. Once I was warmed up and moving along just fine, I would wonder, "Why did I hesitate? That wasn't so bad."

Avoid the Plunge . . .

I have talked with other folks about swimming. They were often impressed that I could swim for a mile. (Honestly, I don't look very athletic—never have.) I will admit, it does require some stamina. But even worse, it can be fairly boring. You are completely alone with your thoughts—and the water. But that's what makes it such great reflective time for me.

I know lots of people who love the summer. They talk about getting back to the water. They do enjoy the beach or the poolside. They love sitting around on a hot day in a brand-new swimsuit. They love dangling their legs in the pool or walking alongside the water of a lake or the waves of the ocean. But they are the first to admit that they don't actually swim.

Sometimes I think life is like that.

We kick around ideas of what we might do. We might pick up a self-help magazine or watch a documentary. We might download part of a Web site. But life is not washing over us in any dramatic way.

We're still just dangling our legs, gently absorbing the scenery, pretending to be engaged in life.

Maybe there's an issue we care about. Maybe we admire the work our friend so-and-so is doing with such-and-such organization. Maybe we wish we could have that kind of passion in our belly. But for some reason, we don't want to dive in and commit. So we stand at the water's edge, and we hesitate. Or we dip our toe in and pretend we are involved. We buy a nice new bathing suit, so we look serious. But we hesitate at the edge. We are unsure. We worry. What will it feel like once we're up to our necks in it, and the only thing to do is kick-kick-kick our way through it?

Maybe we still have some issues. **Maybe we know something powerful is just below the surface, still**

threatening us, frightening us, paralyzing us. Perhaps something happened a long time ago, but we still can't face it. Maybe we are trapped in our own prison by refusing to do the internal work that's necessary to free ourselves. Maybe I need to forgive someone who tried to ruin my life. Maybe I need to let go of someone or something that was taken away.

Whatever it is, ignoring it will never make it go away. It will just keep growing larger and larger until it takes over—kind of like a cancer.

Because the World Is Cancerous . . .

In many ways, the real world can seem like a body with cancer. Everything can work together quite smoothly until a few arrogant and powerful cells start to think they own the place. They can manipulate other cells to join their dark side, and they are so greedy that they don't care what kind of damage they do. They are never satisfied; they always want more and more and more.

All the healthy cells in the body, the good ones, are doing their job, not getting noticed for the most part, but they can't compete anymore. These new hot-shot cancer cells are calling all the plays. They make everyone miserable, and they think they have conquered the world. Except the world they live in is one person's human body.

And sooner or later, they go too far. They won't listen to the warnings. Eventually, the healthy cells have no choice; they must do everything possible to kill off this deadly enemy, even if the friendly fire and collateral damage is way more than we should be risking. We get out the big guns.

We start blowing up cancer cells with radiation and chemotherapy until both sides are ready to surrender.

The cancer will finally realize the folly of its ways, but by then it will be too late. So much damage has been done, the world—this human body—is no longer safe to inhabit. It can no longer sustain life as we know it. The cancer has indeed been victorious, but where is its victory? In defeating all the other cells in the planet, it has destroyed the entire planet as well. The cancer will die along with every other cell in the body.

Well, we hope that the real world isn't as violent as a cancer turned loose in a human body, but you can see the comparison. Call it the mob, call it organized terrorists, call it double agents; cancer is tough to beat when we let it go too far.

. . . and Miss Your Life

However, the way we hesitate at the water's edge before taking the plunge is similar to the way we hesitate before getting truly involved with life. Sometimes we feel as if there is some deadly cancer force out there, and it will drag us down and defeat us, so why bother even trying?

The simplest reason is merely this: We are human beings. We have a responsibility to participate.

If there is anything we will regret at the end of our lives, it will be the times we could have done something but instead chose to do nothing.

Initial hesitation is good. It means you are taking your role seriously. You know it's not a picnic out there. But there comes a time to throw your towel aside and face the water. Even though you know it's not going to be pleasant, at least not at first, it's something you are being called to do. It will shock your system, but the time for standing at the water's edge is over.

You need to plunge in.

You need the waves to knock you silly. You need to kick, kick, kick—and keep breathing—and stretch, stretch, stretch until you start to connect with the world in a meaningful way. That's how you find out what you're really made of. You might surprise yourself.

Things Don't Have to Be Perfect

When I was a kid, and I baked cookies with my mom, we always seemed to burn the last batch. Not on purpose, but just because it signaled the end of the cooking and the beginning of the cleaning up. We started to focus on washing the other baking pans, cleaning up the crumbs, getting out the cookie tins, washing up the measuring cups and spoons, and all of a sudden, we'd smell the last batch starting to burn, and we'd laugh because this seemed to be the pattern we kept repeating.

"Oh well," my mom would say, **"Things don't have to be perfect in order to be wonderful."**

That's one of the most important lessons my mom ever taught me. Not that we need an excuse to be lazy, but we are human after all, and even when we do our best, things can get overlooked. Stuff happens. We can't control everything.

My mom and I would laugh about two sayings that truly balance each other out.

1. Anything worth doing is worth doing well.

Of course. Don't start vast projects with only half-vast ideas. Think about it. Know your situation. Bring in the experts. Talk with your peers. Consider your options. Weigh the pros and cons. Think about the consequences. Choose your solution wisely. Plan well. Follow through. Be thorough.

2. Anything worth doing is worth doing badly.

However, if you are going to wait for things to be perfect, you'll never get anything done at all.

Don't wait for perfection; wonderful is good enough.

Many times, when I was spending a long weekend visiting my nieces (Bernadette, my goddaughter, her sister Barbara, and their cousin Elizabeth), we would talk about what we wanted to do. **There were always more ideas than hours in the day**, so it became a tradition for me to make a list with them. We'd go over the list, decide what our favorite things were, figure out how long each activity might take, add in the hours for eating, driving, and so on, and it became a math problem for us to solve. It was no longer "Aunt Lisa saying no." It became all of us trying to figure it out together.

I was visiting the New Jersey Calderones the weekend of my mom's last Easter, when she was living at Peggy House. It seemed to my niece Barbara that I was spending all my time with her grandma and none of it with her. (She had even asked her older sister Bernadette if she thought Aunt Lisa would keep visiting once Grandma had died. Doesn't that almost break your heart?)

At one point, she came to me and told me she had made a list of all the things she wanted to do with me, and we hadn't found the time to do even one thing on the list. I was so touched by this.

I said, "You made a list for me?" She nodded, with tears in her eyes.

I started tearing up, too.

Together we sat on the floor and looked over her list.

I asked her to tell me the three most important items on the list, and she pointed to them.

We found a way to work in those three, and a couple more. One of them, dying Easter eggs, we did at Peggy House with Grandma.

I told Barbara I was sorry that things were so difficult these days with Grandma. We just can't seem to have perfect visits, because Grandma needs us in a different way now. Barbara must have learned the same lesson I learned from the same wise woman, because she said to me, "I know, Aunt Lisa. Things can't be perfect. But they can still be wonderful."

Tomorrow's Present is the story of how I came to the water's edge and finally dove in.

Starting it was a risky decision, leaving my job and trying to find the money to support a nonprofit. However, I knew it was exactly what I wanted to do with my life. Nothing else called to me more than the idea of spreading the good news about youth leadership; no other cause seemed more important or more exciting. I was completely dedicated to this. I studied it, wrote articles and books about it, and gave workshops all over the United States and Canada about it. Besides, I had so much fun with these leadership teenagers and the adults who assisted us that I could not imagine a better life.

So actually, it wasn't risky at all.
Sometimes, you really, truly know where you belong in life.
You know exactly what you need to do.

Tomorrow is present for you and because you are a present—a gift—to me from tomorrow. I won't make it much further into the future, but you will. And because you are reading my words, you get to take me with you into the future of this world, the future you will help create.

This I Believe

A few years back, I had all the teen leaders at House of Peace write "This I Believe" statements. I wanted them to consider their deepest feelings, most cherished core values, and strongest opinions.

Of course, I had to write my own. This is what I wrote; it was all about them:

I believe in teenagers.

- They won't tolerate boredom, so they encourage fun and laughter.
- They can always spot a phony, so they demand authenticity. If we can't keep it real, we can't be keeping it.

I believe in teenagers.

- Teenagers are old enough to understand the problems that earlier generations have caused, but they're still young enough to have hope.
- They are too old to be shielded from the truth but too young to be completely cynical or apathetic.
- I believe in teenagers because they believe they can make a difference. And they are right.

What do all these teenagers have in common?

- Squeaky-clean youths in private suburban schools, whose parents choose their college by the time they are in kindergarten.

- Rural youths who can drive the family tractor at age ten and don't mind getting dirty or eating pork chops from the pig they raised as a family pet.

- Military youths who answer "Yes, ma'am" or "No, ma'am" to everything you say.

- Urban youths who pass yellow police tape at crime scenes on their way to the bus stop to get to school.

What *could* they all have in common?

They are ready to live. Whether I meet them in schools, or churches, or organizations, they are ready. Young people are eager to learn about their world, reflect on their learning, plan out their response, and put it into practice with community service. They are hungry for mentors and positive peers to support them.

I believe young people are *tomorrow's present* to us.

- They are a gift from the future, a gift we can receive today.

- They are a treasure, because they are young and I am getting older.

- They are energetic while I have weary bones and aching muscles.

- I may have wisdom, but they have enthusiasm.

They infect me with their faith and their confidence, and before I know it, they have me believing in their ideas and visions. They have become leaders.

So, because of teenagers, I believe tomorrow's present for us now. In many ways, tomorrow is already here. I can see their dreams becoming reality. I can perceive glimpses of the future they are creating. It will be better—and cleaner, and safer, and more beautiful, and more peaceful. And with their help, I can be a part of it today. Not only because of what I teach them, but even more so, because of what they teach me.

This I believe:
Because of teenagers, tomorrow's
present.
Because teenagers *are* tomorrow's
present.

My prayer for you is that you find the kind of life work that warms your heart and makes you feel complete. It might not be your job; it might be one of your hobbies. But you will recognize it when you're engaged in it and when you are not.

Even more important, I wish you love and support. May you find your soul mate, if that's who you are looking for. May you find a few mentors (older and wiser) to help guide you. And may you be blessed with good friends and family members who will always delight in your gifts and find ways to make up for your limitations.

Please stay curious.

Ask questions, and learn from every experience, every mistake, and every argument. Learn especially from people with ideas and life experiences completely different from yours.

Please, reflect on everything you learn.

Discover your passions, your God-given talents, and find a way to live out your most cherished values. Work out your issues. Be quick to forgive and slow to condemn. Believe in the goodness and potential of all people. Make time to enjoy your loved ones.

Please make careful decisions based on your values, after hearing advice from those at the top and at the bottom.

Lead with integrity, speak honestly, and earn the trust and respect of your peers. That way, when you do make mistakes, people will be more forgiving and less likely to question your motivation.

Please serve the needs of others.

Avoid the trappings of greed and power; look beyond a person's appearance so you see into the soul. Resolve to find ways to keep improving your life and your community. Be sure that justice is your overall goal. Accept your defeats with grace and your victories with humility. **Let your hope be contagious. Be happy.**

You can learn more by visiting the Tomorrow's Present Web site at http://www.tomorrowspresent.org.

12

Get Ready to Die

I remember reading an *Arlo and Janis* comic strip a few years ago. Gene, a middle schooler, was complaining to his friend about his mom, who had just bought him his first suit. The sales clerk at the store had said that it would "make a good suit for a funeral." He was especially annoyed that his mother agreed, saying, "Yes, that's always good."

He asked his friend, "What is it with grown-ups? It's as if they expect people to die."

This strip really captures the sense of the young; some of them haven't completely realized that everyone does indeed die.

Not all teens are afraid to talk about death. An e-mail from my niece Bernadette, who was a high school junior at the time, brought tears to my eyes. She wrote:

> "The way you're dying is peaceful, and it doesn't make it as hard for the rest of the world. I love the way you're leaving gracefully—it fits you perfectly and is really beautiful."

Life with terminal cancer is like having a ticking bomb inside my body, set to go off at some unknown time in the next few months. The major warning signs are harsh pain, especially after eating, yellowish skin and eyes (jaundice) and a few other symptoms I don't think I'll mention.

The journey isn't smooth or linear. I can feel worse, then a little better, then get even worse again, then maybe a tad better again for awhile. **So when the pain does**

get harsh, I never know if that means a bump in the road . . . or the end of the road.

Because of that, I don't take anything for granted. Not a person, not a sunrise, not a single bite of food or cup of tea. Everything becomes a blessing, because every last visit or phone call could indeed turn out to be my very last visit or phone call.

Honeymoon Phase of Cancer

People have asked me to describe what it's like having cancer. I have often talked about a process of several phases, such as the first phase, "the honeymoon" phase of cancer.

The honeymoon phase is when things are still fairly normal: relatively little pain, some manageable fatigue, and a good bit of independence. Everyone is attentive to your needs, bending over backward to assist with every little thing. There are many gatherings with family and friends, with laughter, the sharing of stories, and easy affection—everyone saying how marvelous you are, what a genius you are, how talented and beautiful. It's fabulous.

Who wouldn't love such an endless party?

Basically, it's the economics of dying; your perceived supply goes down (decrease in the overall number of times to see Lisa), so your perceived demand goes up ("We've gotta see Lisa! Who knows when it will be our last chance?").

I often thought, *"So far, this cancer gig isn't too bad."* In fact, I had so much fun celebrating with the people I love, that I kept telling them my "dying thing" had been the best part of my whole "living thing."

Well, the honeymoon is over.

Middle Phase of Cancer

Don't get me wrong. People are still attentive, and I am still being treated like royalty. But I have entered the middle phase of cancer (I hope you realize that I am making up these names and phases). **I am less independent, and my constant dull pain keeps me uncomfortable all the time.**

The middle phase is when you haven't yet begun to suffer the worst pain, or the most devastating loss of body functions, or the will to live another day. However, you are obviously declining.

The middle phase is when you can still pretend to be winning; you're still able to keep a couple of steps ahead. The cancer hasn't beaten you yet, but it's close enough that you can smell it coming. You hear its footsteps and can see it in your rearview mirror, along with the warning that objects are closer than they appear. Pretty soon, you are going to feel its hot breath at the back of your neck.

And that next phase is not going to be easy, or fun, or romantic, or noble. It will be downright ugly. In fact, I have named it the ugly phase.

Ugly Phase of Cancer

It could be horribly unpleasant at best, and downright hellish at worst. The pain will be much worse, maybe excruciating. **I will have lost most of my energy, all my sparkling personality, and much of my independence.** I've already begun to imagine all the smelly stuff I can look forward to as my body deteriorates—things to embarrass me, test my patience, and leave me feeling helpless and hopeless. I might wish for death to come quickly. All of this is normal as the cancer grows in physical size and emotional importance. Soon, it will seem to fill up my entire home.

Imagine what the ugly phase will be like for my friends and family. I don't have a choice, but they do. They could shut it all out. They could stop visiting and calling. They could become emotionally unavailable and avoid this whole mess.

Who could blame them?

The ugly phase is when you are no longer good company, and most people have stopped visiting.

They don't have much to say, and neither do you. (This can be a good thing because visits are exhausting.)

By then, all the visitors can do is sit quietly while you nap and smile when you open your eyes. Sometimes they hold your hand and you might remember what love feels like.

Imagine the caregivers. Usually they are close family; sometimes they include close friends. In spite of great love, I realize that it's normal for caregivers to develop feelings of resentment and bitterness as they deal with the frustration and inconvenience. **Some of them might even wish at times that I was already dead, and then they feel guilty for wishing it.** They might get tired of having my needs interrupt their personal lives and schedules. They could well grow weary of the "urgency" of my upcoming death. And they will not want to complain, because after all, they are the ones staying alive.

And by then, I might be unable to console them, or comfort them, or say, "It's OK for you to have those feelings. It's normal. You've done so much for me, and still I require more. I'm so sorry. It wasn't my choice. I didn't want to become a burden. I can't help it. **But thank you, once again, for choosing to love me and take care of me.** I feel so undeserving. Your love means everything to me. What would I do without you?"

I want to say it all now, because I know, eventually, when they will most need to hear it, I won't be able to say it.

Death in Phases

I'm sure of one more phase, the final phase, when you are no longer aware of your situation. You sleep most of the time, or you're unconscious. When people do come, it looks and feels more like a wake, with people whispering to one another as you rest, eyes closed, in their midst.

That's it: the honeymoon phase, the middle phase, the ugly phase, and the final phase.

That's how things play out. Not always, but often. **Some people are lucky.** They go straight from the honeymoon phase to the final phase. Most of us don't. (It usually happens that way only in the movies.)

What is it that makes our friends and family so willing to say yes, despite the ugliness that terminal illness brings? How can they continue to love you when almost everything that made you lovable and delightful disappears?

It's one of those great mysteries of life.

When People Are Like God

When people love us that fiercely, they are so very much like God.

The less "lovable" their loved one seems, the more they resemble God in loving us anyway. What a blessing, especially when we feel so unworthy.

Autumn has finally arrived.

It's time to keep the windows open—cool enough during the day to provide a gentle breeze and crisp enough to enjoy pulling the covers up at night.

This is the time of year when you don't need heating or air conditioning. At lunchtime, I can hear children playing in the school yard. **With the windows open, the church bells across the street sound louder and more joyful.**

It's a glorious time. Fall is my favorite season. When you are dying during the fall, it's almost impossible to avoid the symbolism of the trees; just before their leaves die, they become the most gorgeous of all, in brilliant shades of gold and crimson.

Obviously, that means we are most gorgeous and brilliant as we approach the end of our lives . . . right?

I don't have the energy to argue with that conclusion; I feel as old and tired as that cliché. But ask me if I feel brilliant and gorgeous, and I bet you could guess my answer.

Yet we do become wiser as we age.

Wise enough to actually have good advice to give, but smart enough to keep quiet until someone asks our opinion.

In the Bible, there is a famous passage that has inspired me. Here's my version:

> There is an appointed time for everything, a
>   season for every task under heaven:
> A time to weep and grieve; and a time to laugh
>   and dance,
> A time to be silent and let your children make
>   their own mistakes,
> and a time to shout at them so they notice the
>   cars on the street and remain on the side-
>   walk.
> A time to play it safe, and a time to take risks.
> A time to insist that the kids dress warmly, and
>   a time to let them go out poorly dressed so
>   they feel the cold and learn that weather
>   must influence clothing choice.
> A time to splurge on a special dinner, and a
>   time to stretch the leftovers.

A time to check their homework and help
    them study,
and a time to let them learn that sloppy work
    earns a lower grade.
A time to say, "I'm sorry; you were right and I
    was wrong,"
and a time to flash your "I told you so" smile.
A time to be born, and a time to die.
A time to say, "I love you,"
and a time to say, "I love you."

The real mystery of autumn is this:

What does the green leaf, still firmly attached to the tree, need to know from the crinkled-up brown one, seconds before the wind snatches it off and whirls it away?

What could the brown one possibly have to offer?

Other than this:

> "The best part of my life has been
> the honor of sharing this tree branch
> with you . . ."

Thank you.

Lisa's Prayer

I pray that you will live a life of justice,
protecting the rights of those who have no power.
I pray you know the presence of the Christ
and feel him with you in your final hour.
I pray that you will breathe the air of freedom
and wisely exercise your vote and voice;
and heed the Spirit's guidance in decisions,
and seek the will of God in every choice.
I pray that you will always love your neighbor
and be sensitive to hurts too deep to share.
I pray you learn to listen to the suffering
and treat the helpless with respect and care.
I pray that you are one with all Creation
and stand in awe of Nature every day.
I pray you humbly bow to your Creator.
I simply pray that you will always pray.

Continue the Conversation

If you enjoyed this book, then connect with Loyola Press to continue the conversation, engage with other readers, and find out about new and upcoming books from your favorite spiritual writers.

Visit us at
www.LoyolaPress.com
to create an account and register for our newsletters.

Or you can just click on the code to the right with your smartphone to sign up.

Connect with us on the following:

Facebook
facebook.com/loyolapress

Twitter
twitter.com/loyolapress

You Tube
youtube.com/loyolapress

Making a Difference in the World
One Person at a Time

Thrift Store Saints
Meeting Jesus 25¢ at a Time
Jane Knuth

$13.95 • Pb • 3301-2

Thrift Store Saints is a collection of true stories based on Jane Knuth's experiences serving the poor at a St. Vincent de Paul thrift store in the inner city of Kalamazoo, Michigan. This book makes clear that you don't need to be a heroic Mother Teresa-type to make a difference with the poor. The stories in **Thrift Store Graces** subtly compel us to redefine what it means to volunteer.

Thrift Store Graces
Finding God's Gifts in the Midst of the Mess
Jane Knuth

$13.95 • Pb • 3692-1

In **Thrift Store Graces**, Knuth introduces us to some far more challenging personal situations that emerge as a result of her volunteer work—at the Kalamazoo thrift store. Additionally, she invites us to join her as she hesitantly embarks on a pilgrimage to Medjugorje in war-torn Bosnia. Witty, inspiring, and thought-provoking all at once, the stories in **Thrift Store Graces** subtly compel us to redefine what it means to volunteer and to rethink why it is that we volunteer in the first place.

To order: call 800-621-1008, or visit www.loyolapress.com/store or visit your local bookseller.